THE DECORATIVE ILLUSTRATION OF BOOKS. BY WALTER CRANE.

OF THE DECORATIVE ILLUSTRATION OF BOOKS OLD AND NEW BY WALTER CRANE ❦

LONDON: GEORGE BELL AND SONS
YORK HOUSE, PORTUGAL STREET, W.C.
NEW YORK: 66 FIFTH AVENUE
MDCCCCV

REPUBLISHED BY GALE RESEARCH COMPANY, BOOK TOWER, DETROIT, 1968

Library of Congress Catalog Card Number 68–30611

HIS book had its origin in the course of three (Cantor) Lectures given before the Society of Arts in 1889; they have been amplified and added to, and further chapters have been written, treating of the very active period in printing and decorative book-illustration we have seen since that time, as well as some remarks and suggestions touching the general principles and conditions governing the design of book pages and ornaments.

It is not nearly so complete or comprehensive as I could have wished, but there are natural limits to the bulk of a volume in the "Ex-Libris" series, and it has been only possible to carry on such a work in the intervals snatched from the absorbing work of designing. Within its own lines, however, I hope that if not exhaustive, the book may be found fairly representative of the chief historical and contemporary types of decorative book-illustration.

In the selection of the illustrations, I have endeavoured to draw the line between the purely graphic aim, on the one hand, and the ornamental aim on the other—between what I should term the art of *pictorial statement* and the art of *decorative treatment;* though there are many cases in which they are combined, as, indeed, in all the most complete book-pictures, they should be. My purpose has been to treat of illustrations which are also book-ornaments, so that purely graphic design, as such, unrelated to the type, and the conditions of the page, does not come within my scope.

As book-illustration pure and simple, however, has been treated of in this series by Mr. Joseph

PREFACE.

Pennell, whose selection is more from the graphic than the decorative point of view, the balance may be said to be adjusted as regards contemporary art.

I must offer my best thanks to Mr. Gleeson White, without whose most valuable help the book might never have been finished. He has allowed me to draw upon his remarkable collection of modern illustrated books for examples, and I am indebted to many artists for permission to use their illustrations, as well as to Messrs. George Allen, Bradbury, Agnew and Co., J. M. Dent and Co., Edmund Evans, Geddes and Co., Hacon and Ricketts (the Vale Press), John Lane, Lawrence and Bullen, Sampson Low and Co., Macmillan and Co., Elkin Mathews, Kegan Paul and Co., Walter Scott, Charles Scribner's Sons, and Virtue and Co., for their courtesy in giving me, in many cases, the use of the actual blocks.

To Mr. William Morris, who placed his beautiful collection of early printed books at my disposal, from which to choose illustrations ; to Mr. Emery Walker for help in many ways ; to Mr. John Calvert for permission to use some of his father's illustrations ; and to Mr. A. W. Pollard who has lent me some of his early Italian examples, and has also supervised my bibliographical particulars, I desire to make my cordial acknowledgments.

WALTER CRANE.

Kensington : *July 18th,* 1896.

vi

REPRINT of this book being called for, I take the opportunity of adding a few notes, chiefly to Chapter IV., which will be found further on with the numbers of the pages to which they refer.

As touching the general subject of the book one may, perhaps, be allowed to record with some satisfaction that the study of lettering, text-writing, and illumination is now seriously taken up in our craft-schools. The admirable teaching of Mr. Johnston of the Central School of Arts and Crafts and the Royal College of Art in this connection cannot be too highly spoken of. We have had, too, admirable work, in each kind, from Mr. Reuter, Mr. Mortimer, Mr. Treglown, Mr. Alan Vigers, Mr. Graily Hewitt, and Mr. A. E. R. Gill; and Mrs. Traguair and Miss Kingsford are remarkable for the beauty, delicacy, and invention of their work as illuminators among the artists who are now pursuing this beautiful branch of art.

So that the ancient crafts of the scribe and illuminator may be said to have again come to life, and this, taken in connection with the revival of printing as an art, is an interesting and significant fact.

As recent contributions to the study of lettering we have Mr. Lewis F. Day's recent book of Alphabets, and Mr. G. Woolliscroft Rhead's sheets for school use.

I have to deplore the loss of my former helper in this book, Mr. Gleeson White, since the work first appeared. His extensive knowledge of, and sympathy with the modern book illustrators of the younger generation was remarkable, and as a designer himself he showed considerable skill and taste in book-decoration, chiefly in the way of covers. As a most estimable and amiable character he will always be remembered by his friends.

WALTER CRANE.

KENSINGTON: *June*, 1904.

CONTENTS.

CHAPTER I.—OF THE EVOLUTION OF THE ILLUSTRATIVE AND DECORATIVE IMPULSE FROM THE EARLIEST TIMES; AND OF THE FIRST PERIOD OF DECORATIVELY ILLUSTRATED BOOKS IN THE ILLUMINATED MSS. OF THE MIDDLE AGES. 1.

CHAPTER II.—OF THE TRANSITION, AND OF THE SECOND PERIOD OF DECORATIVELY ILLUSTRATED BOOKS, FROM THE INVENTION OF PRINTING IN THE FIFTEENTH CENTURY ONWARDS. 45.

CHAPTER III.—OF THE PERIOD OF THE DECLINE OF DECORATIVE FEELING IN BOOK DESIGN AFTER THE SIXTEENTH CENTURY, AND OF THE MODERN REVIVAL. 125.

CHAPTER IV.—OF RECENT DEVELOPMENT OF DECORATIVE BOOK ILLUSTRATION, AND THE MODERN REVIVAL OF PRINTING AS AN ART. 185.

CHAPTER V.—OF GENERAL PRINCIPLES IN DESIGNING BOOK ORNAMENTS AND ILLUSTRATIONS: CONSIDERATION OF ARRANGEMENT, SPACING AND TREATMENT. 279.

INDEX. 329.

LIST OF ILLUSTRATIONS.

GERMAN SCHOOL, XVTH CENTURY.   PAGE

"Leiden Christi." (Bamberg, 1470)   3
Boccaccio, "De Claris Mulieribus." (Ulm, 1473) . 7, 11
"Buch von den sieben Todsünden." (Augsburg,
    1474)   15
"Speculum Humanæ Vitæ." Augsburg, *cir.* 1475) 17
Bible. (Cologne, 1480)   21
Terrence : "Eunuchus." (Ulm, 1486)   27
"Chronica Hungariæ." (Augsburg, 1488) . . .   35
"Hortus Sanitatis." (Mainz, 1491)   39
"Chroneken der Sassen." (Mainz, 1492) . . .   41
Bible. (Lubeck, 1494)   47
"Æsop's Fables." (Ulm, 1498).   53

FLEMISH AND DUTCH SCHOOLS, XVTH CENTURY.

"Spiegel onser Behoudenisse." (Kuilenburg, 1483) 25
"Life of Christ." (Antwerp, 1487).   31

FRENCH SCHOOL, XVTH CENTURY.

"La Mer des Histoires." Initial. (Paris, 1488) . 37
"Paris et Vienne." (Paris, *cir.* 1495) 51

ITALIAN SCHOOL, XVTH CENTURY.

"De Claris Mulieribus." (Ferrara, 1497). . . .   54
Tuppo's "Æsop." (Naples, 1485)   55
P. Cremonese's "Dante." (Venice, 1491) . . .   56
"Discovery of the Indies." (Florence, 1493) . .   57
"Fior di Virtù." (Florence, 1498)   58
Stephanus Caesenas: "Expositio Beati Hieronymi in
    Psalterium." (Venice, 1498)   59
"Poliphili Hypnerotomachia." (Venice, 1499) . 63, 65
Ketham's "Fasciculus Medicinæ." (Venice, 1493) 295
Pomponius Mela. (Venice, 1478)   297

ITALIAN SCHOOL, XVITH CENTURY.

Artist Unknown. Bernadino Corio. (Milan, Minu-
    ziano, 1503)   67
School of Bellini : "Supplementum Supplementi
    Chronicarum, etc." (Venice, 1506)   69
"The Descent of Minerva": from the Quatriregio.
    (Florence, 1508)   71
Aulus Gellius. (Venice, 1509)   73
Quintilian. (Venice, 1512)   75

LIST OF ILLUSTRATIONS.

ITALIAN SCHOOL, XVITH CENTURY—*continued.*   PAGE

Ottaviano dei Petrucci. (Fossombrone, 1513) . .   77

Ambrosius Calepinus. (Tosculano, 1520) . . .   121

Artist unknown : Portrait title : Ludovico Dolci, 1561. (Venice, Giolito, 1562)   133

GERMAN SCHOOL, XVITH CENTURY.

Albrecht Dürer : " Kleine Passion." (Nuremberg, 1512) 81, 83, 85

Albrecht Dürer : " Plutarchus Chaeroneus." (Nuremberg, 1513)   87

Albrecht Dürer : " Plutarchus Chaeroneus." (Nuremberg, 1523)   89

Hans Holbein : " Dance of Death." (Lyons, 1538) 91, 92

Hans Holbein : Title-page : Gallia. (Basel, *cir.* 1524)   93

Hans Holbein : Bible Cuts. (Lyons, 1538) . . 95, 96

Ambrose Holbein : " Neues Testament." (Basel, 1523)   97

Hans Burgmair : " Der Weiss König." (1512-14) .   99

Hans Burgmair : " Iornandes de Rebus Gothorum." (Augsburg, 1516)   101

Hans Burgmair : " Pliny's Natural History." (Frankfort, 1582)   103

Hans Burgmair : " Meerfahrt zu viln onerkannten Inseln," etc. (Augsburg, 1509)   105

Hans Baldung Grün : " Hortulus Animæ." (Strassburg, 1511) 107, 108, 109, 110

Hans Wächtlin : Title Page. (Strassburg, 1513) .   111

Hans Sebald Beham : " Das Papstthum mit seinen Gliedern." (Nuremberg, 1526)   113

Reformation der bayrischen Landrecht. (Munich, 1518)   117

Fuchsius : " De Historia Stirpium." (Basel, 1542) .   123

Virgil Solis : Bible. (Frankfort, 1563)   131

Johann Otmar : " Pomerium de Tempore." (Augsburg, 1502)   147

FRENCH SCHOOL, XVITH CENTURY.

Oronce Finé : " Quadrans Astrolabicus." (Paris, 1534)   127

MODERN ILLUSTRATION.

William Blake : " Songs of Innocence," 1789 . .   137

xi

LIST OF ILLUSTRATIONS.

MODERN ILLUSTRATION—*continued*.   PAGE

William Blake: "Phillip's Pastoral" 139

Edward Calvert: Original Woodcuts: "The Lady
and the Rooks," "The Return Home," "Chamber
Idyll," "The Flood," "Ideal Pastoral Life,"
"The Brook," 1827-29 . . . . 141, 143

Dante Gabriel Rossetti: "Tennyson's Poems," 1857   151

Dante Gabriel Rossetti: "Early Italian Poets," 1861   153

Albert Moore: "Milton's Ode on the Nativity,"
1867 155

Henry Holiday: Cover for "Aglaia," 1893 . . . 157

Randolph Caldecott: Headpiece to "Bracebridge
Hall," 1877 158

Kate Greenaway: Title Page of "Mother Goose" . 159

Arthur Hughes: "At the Back of the North Wind,"
1871 . . . . 160, 161

Arthur Hughes: "Mercy" ("Good Words for the
Young," 1871) 304

Robert Bateman: "Art in the House," 1876. . . 162,
163, 164, 165

Heywood Sumner: Peard's "Stories for Children,"
1896 . . . . 167, 170

Charles Keene: "A Good Fight." ("Once a
Week," 1859) 169

Louis Davis: "Sleep, Baby, Sleep" ("English Illustrated Magazine," 1892) 171

Henry Ryland: "Forget not yet" ("English Illustrated Magazine," 1894) 173

Frederick Sandys: "The Old Chartist" ("Once a
Week," 1861) 175

M. J. Lawless: "Dead Love" ("Once a Week,"
1862) 177

Walter Crane: Grimm's "Household Stories," 1882   179

Walter Crane: "Princess Fiorimonde," 1880 . . 181

Walter Crane: "The Sirens Three," 1886 . . . 183

Selwyn Image: "Scottish Art Review," 1889 . . 187

William Morris and Walter Crane: "The Glittering
Plain," 1894 . . . . 191, 290, 291

C. M. Gere: "Midsummer" ("English Illustrated
Magazine," 1893) 195

C. M. Gere: "The Birth of St. George" 197

Arthur Gaskin: "Hans Andersen," 1893 199

xii

MODERN ILLUSTRATION—*continued.*   PAGE

E. H. New: "Bridge Street, Evesham" 201

Inigo Thomas: "The Formal Garden," 1892 . 204, 205

Henry Payne: "A Book of Carols," 1893. . . . 209

F. Mason: "Huon of Bordeaux," 1895 211

Gertrude, M. Bradley: "The Cherry Festival," . . 213

Mary Newill: Porlock 215

Celia Levetus: A Bookplate 217

C. S. Ricketts: "Hero and Leander," 1894 . . . 219

C. S. Ricketts: "Daphnis and Chloe," 1893 . . . 223

C. H. Shannon: "Daphnis and Chloe," 1893 . . 224

Aubrey Beardsley: 'Morte d'Arthur," 1893 225, 226, 227

Edmund J. Sullivan: "Sartor Resartus," 1898 . . 228

Patten Wilson: A Pen Drawing 229

Laurence Housman: "The House of Joy," 1895 . 231

L. Fairfax Muckley: "Frangilla" 233

Charles Robinson: "A Child's Garden of Verse,"
    1895 . . . . 235, 237, 239

J. D. Batten: "The Arabian Nights," 1893 .   241, 242

R. Anning Bell: "A Midsummer Night's Dream,"
    1895 243

R. Anning Bell: "Beauty and the Beast," 1894 . 245

R. Spence: A Pen Drawing 247

A. Garth Jones: "A Tournament of Love," 1894 . 249

William Strang: "Baron Munchausen," 1895 . 251, 253

H. Granville Fell: "Cinderella," 1894 254

John Duncan: "Apollo's Schooldays" ("The Ever-
    green," 1895) 255

John Duncan: "Pipes of Arcady" ("The Ever-
    green," 1895) 257

Robert Burns: "The Passer-By" ("The Evergreen,"
    1895) 259

Mary Sargant Florence: "The Crystal Ball," 1894 . 261

Paul Woodroffe: "Ye Second Book of Nursery
    Rhymes," 1896 263

Paul Woodroffe: "Ye Book of Nursery Rhymes," 1895 265

M. Rijsselberghe: "Dietrich's Almanack," 1894 . 266

Walter Crane: "Spenser's Faerie Queen," 1896 . 269,
                  281, 233, 285

Howard Pyle: "Otto of the Silver Hand" . 271, 273

Will. H. Bradley: Covers for "The Inland Printer,"
    1894 274

LIST OF ILLUSTRATIONS.

MODERN ILLUSTRATION—*continued*.   PAGE

    Will. H. Bradley: Prospectus for "Bradley His
        Book," 1896 275

    Will. H. Bradley: Design for "The Chap Book,"
        1895 277

    Alan Wright: Headpieces from "The Story of My
        House," 1892 . . . . 305, 335

    The untitled tailpieces throughout this volume are
        from Grimm's "Household Stories," illustrated
        by Walter Crane. (Macmillan, 1882.)

APPENDIX OF HALF-TONE BLOCKS.

    I. Book of Kells. Irish, VIth century.

    II., III., IV. Arundel Psalter. English, XIVth century.
        (Arundel MSS. 83 B. M.)

    V. Epistle of Phillipe de Comines to Richard II. French,
        XIVth century. (Royal MSS. 20 B. vi. B. M.)

    VI., VII. Bedford Hours. (MSS. 18, 850 B. M.)

    VIII. Romance of the Rose. English, late XVth century.
        (Hast. MSS. 4, 425.)

    IX. Choir Book. Siena. Italian, XVth century.

    X., XI. Hokusai. Japanese, XIXth century.

CHAPTER I. OF THE EVOLUTION OF THE ILLUSTRATIVE AND DECORATIVE IMPULSE FROM THE EARLIEST TIMES; AND OF THE FIRST PERIOD OF DECORATIVELY ILLUSTRATED BOOKS IN THE ILLUMINATED MSS. OF THE MIDDLE AGES.

Y subject is a large one, and touches more intimately, perhaps, than other forms of art, both human thought and history, so that it would be extremely difficult to treat it exhaustively upon all its sides. I shall not attempt to deal with it from the historical or antiquarian points of view more than may be necessary to elucidate the artistic side, on which I propose chiefly to approach the question of design as applied to books—or, more strictly, the book page—which I shall hope to illustrate by reproductions of characteristic examples from different ages and countries.

I may, at least, claim to have been occupied, in a practical sense, with the subject more or less, as part of my work, both as a decorator and illustrator of books, for the greater part of my life, and such conclusions as I have arrived at are based upon the results of personal thought and experience, if they are also naturally coloured and influenced from the same sources.

All forms of art are so closely connected with life and thought, so bound up with human conditions, habits, and customs; so intimately and vividly do they reflect every phase and change of that unceasing movement—the ebb and flow of human progress amid the forces of nature we call history—that it is hardly possible even for the most careless stroller, taking any of the by-paths, not to be led insensibly to speculate on their hidden sources, and an origin perhaps common to them all.

The story of man is fossilized for us, as it were, or rather preserved, with all its semblance of life and colour, in art and books. The procession of history reaching far back into the obscurity of the forgotten or inarticulate past, is reflected, with all its movement, gold and colour, in the limpid stream of design, that mirror-like, paints each passing phase for us, and illustrates each act in the drama. In the language of line and of letters, of symbol and picture, each age writes its own story and character, as page after page is turned in the book of time. Here and there the continuity of the chapters is broken, a page is missing, a passage is obscure; there are breaks and fragments—heroic torsos and limbs instead of whole figures. But more and more, by patient research, labour, and comparison, the voids are being filled up, until some day perhaps there will be no chasm of conjecture in which to plunge, but the volume of art and human history will be as clear as pen and pencil can make it, and only left for a present to continue, and a future to carry to a completion which is yet never complete.

If painting is the looking-glass of nations and periods, pictured-books may be called the hand-glass which still more intimately reflects the life of different centuries and peoples, in all their

LEIDEN CHRISTI.   (BAMBERG, ALBRECHT PFISTER, 1470.)

3

minute and homely detail and quaint domesticity, as well as their playful fancies, their dreams, and aspirations. While the temples and the tombs of ancient times tell us of the pomp and splendour and ambition of kings, and the stories of their conquests and tyrannies, the illuminated MSS. of the Middle Ages show us, as well as these, the more intimate life of the people, their sports and their jests, their whim and fancy, their work and their play, no less than the mystic and religious and ceremonial side of that life, which was, indeed, an inseparable part of it; the whole worked in as with a kind of embroidery of the pen and brush, with the most exquisite sense of decorative beauty.

Mr. Herbert Spencer, in the course of his enunciation of the philosophy of evolution, speaks of the book and the newspaper lying on the table of the modern citizen as connected through a long descent with the hieroglyphic inscriptions of the ancient Egyptians, and the picture-writing of still earlier times. We might go (who knows how much further?) back into prehistoric obscurity to find the first illustrator, pure and simple, in the hunter of the cave, who recorded the incidents of his sporting life on the bones of his victims.

We know that the letters of our alphabet were once pictures, symbols, or abstract signs of entities and actions, and grew more and more abstract until they became arbitrary marks—the familiar characters that we know. Letters formed into words; words increased and multiplied with ideas and their interchange; ideas and words growing more and more abstract until the point is reached when the jaded intellect would fain return again to picture-writing,

5

and welcomes the decorator and the illustrator to relieve the desert wastes of words marshalled in interminable columns on the printed page.

In a journey through a book it is pleasant to reach the oasis of a picture or an ornament, to sit awhile under the palms, to let our thoughts unburdened stray, to drink of other intellectual waters, and to see the ideas we have been pursuing, perchance, reflected in them. Thus we end as we begin, with images.

Temples and tombs have been man's biggest books, but with the development of individual life (as well as religious ritual, and the necessity of records,) he felt the need of something more familiar, companionable, and portable, and having, in the course of time, invented the stylus, and the pen, and tried his hand upon papyrus, palm leaf, and parchment, he wrote his records or his thoughts, and pictured or symbolized them, at first upon scrolls and rolls and tablets, or, later, enshrined them in bound books, with all the beauty that the art of writing could command, enriched and emphasized with the pictorial and ornamental commentary in colours and gold.

As already indicated, it is my purpose to deal with the artistic aspects of the book page, and therefore we are not now concerned with the various forms of the book itself, as such, or with the treatment of its exterior case, cover, or binding. It is the open book I wish to dwell on—the page itself as a field for the designer and illustrator—a space to be made beautiful in design.

Both decorated and illustrated books may be divided broadly into two great periods :

FROM BOCCACCIO, DE CLARIS MULIERIBUS. (ULM, JOHANN ZAINER, 1473.)

7

I. The MS., or period before printing.

II. The period of printed books.

Both illustrate, however, a long course of evolution, and contain in themselves, it might be said, a compendium—or condensation—of the history of contemporary art in its various forms of development. The first impulse in art seems to answer to the primitive imitative impulse in children—the desire to embody the familiar forms about them— to characterize them in line and colour. The salient points of an animal, for instance, being first emphasized—as in the bone scratchings of the cave men—so that children's drawings and drawings of primitive peoples present a certain family likeness, allowing for difference of environment. They are abstract, and often almost symbolic in their characterization of form, and it is not difficult to imagine how letters and written language became naturally evolved through a system of hieroglyphics, starting from the unsystemized but irrepressible tendency of the human to record his linear ideas of rhythm on the one hand, or his impressions of nature on the other. It would seem that the illustrator or picture writer came first in the order of things, and the book afterwards—like the system we have heard of under modern editors of magazines, of the picture being done first and then written up to, or down to, by the author.

Side by side with the evolution of letters and calligraphic art went on the evolution of the graphic power and the artistic sense, developing on the one hand towards close imitation of nature and dramatic incident, and on the other towards imaginative beauty, and systematic, organic ornament,

9

more or less built upon a geometric basis, but ultimately bursting into a free foliation and flamboyant blossom, akin in inventive richness and variety to a growth of nature herself. The development of these two main directions of artistic energy may be followed throughout the whole world of art, constantly struggling, as it were, for the ascendancy, now one and now the other being paramount; but the history of their course, and the effect of their varying influences is particularly marked in the decoration and illustration of books.

Although as a rule the decorative sense was dominant throughout the illuminated books of the Middle Ages, the illustrator, in the form of the miniaturist, is in evidence, and in some, especially in the later MSS., finally conquers, or rather absorbs, the decorator.

There is a MS. in the Egerton collection in the British Museum (No. 943), "The Divina Commedia" of Dante, with miniatures by Italian artists of the fourteenth century, which may be taken as an early instance of the ascendancy of the illustrator, the miniatures being placed somewhat abruptly on the page, and with unusually little framework or associated ornament ; and although more or less decorative in the effect of their simple design, and frank and full colour, the main object of their artists was to illustrate rather than to decorate the text.

The Celtic genius, under the influence of Christianity, and as representing the art of the early Christian Western civilization—exemplified in the remarkable designs in the Book of Kells—was, on the other hand, strictly ornamental in its manifes-

FROM BOCCACCIO, DE CLARIS MULIERIBUS.   (ULM, JOHANN ZAINER, 1473.)

11

tations, suggesting in its richness, and in the intricacy and ingenuity of its involved patterns, as well as the geometric forms of many of its units, a relation to certain characteristics of Eastern as well as primitive Greek art.

The Book of Kells derives its name from the Columban Monastery of Kells or Kenlis, originally Cennanas, a place of ancient importance in the county of Meath, Ireland, and it is supposed to have been the Great Gospel brought to the Christian settlement by its founder, St. Columba, and perhaps written by that saint, who died in the year 597. The original volume is in the library of Trinity College, Dublin.

In one of the pages of this book is represented the Greek monogram of Christ, and the whole page is devoted to three words, Christi Autem Generatio. It is a remarkable instance of an ornamental initial spreading over an entire page. The effect of the whole as a decoration is perhaps what might be called heavy, but it is full of marvellous detail and richness, and highly characteristic of Celtic forms of ornamental design (*see* No. 1, Appendix).

The work of the scribe, as shown in the form of the ordinary letters of the text, is very fine. They are very firm and strong in character, to balance the closely knit and firmly built ornamentation of the initial letters and other ornaments of the pages. We feel that they have a dignity, a distinction, and a character all their own.

There is a page in the same book where the symbols of the evangelists are inclosed in circles, and panelled in a solid framing occupying the whole page, which suggests Byzantine feeling in design.

The full pages in the earlier illuminated MSS. were often panelled out in four or more compartments to hold figures of saints, or emblems, and in the twelfth and thirteenth centuries such panels generally had small patterned diapered backgrounds, on dark blue, red, green, or burnished gold.

The Anglo-Saxon MSS. show traces of the influence of the traditions of Classic art drawn through the Byzantine, or from the Roman sources, which naturally affected the earliest forms of Christian art as we see its relics in the catacombs. These classical traditions are especially noticeable in the treatment of the draperies clinging in linear and elliptical folds to express the limbs. In fact, it might be said that, spread westward and northward by the Christian colonies, this classical tradition in figure design lingered on, until its renewal at the dawn of the Renaissance itself, and the resurrection of classical art in Italy, which, uniting with a new naturalism, grew to that wonderful development which has affected the art of Europe ever since.

The Charter of Foundation of Newminster, at Winchester, by King Edgar, A.D. 966, written in gold, is another very splendid early example of book decoration. It has a full-page miniature of the panelled type above mentioned, and elaborate border in gold and colours by an English artist. It is in the British Museum, and may be seen open in Case 2 in the King's Library.

"The Gospels," in Latin. A MS. of the eleventh century, with initials and borders in gold and colours, by English artists, is another fine specimen of the

14

early kind. Here the titles of each gospel, boldly inscribed, are inclosed in a massively designed

GERMAN SCHOOL. XVth CENTURY.

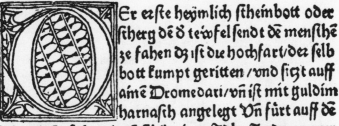

"BUCH VON DEN SIEBEN TODSÜNDEN UND DEN SIEBEN TUGENDEN."
(AUGSBURG, BÄMLER, 1474.)

border, making a series of full title pages of a dignified type.

As examples of illustrated books, according to

the earlier Mediæval ideas, we may look at twelfth
and thirteenth century "Herbals," wherein different
plants, very full and frank in colour and formal in
design, are figured strictly with a view to the ornamentation of the page. There is a very fine one,
described as written in England in the thirteenth
century, in the British Museum. Decoration and
illustration are here one and the same.

A magnificent specimen of book decoration of
the most splendid kind is the "Arundel Psalter"
(Arundel MS. 83, Brit. Mus.), given by Robert de
Lyle to his daughter Audry, as an inscription in
the volume tells us, in 1339. Here scribe, illuminator, and miniaturist are all at their best, whether
one and the same or different persons. It is, moreover, English work. There is no doubt about the
beauty of the designs, and the variety and richness
of the decorative effect. Like all the Psalters, the
book commences with a calendar, and full pages
follow, panelled out and filled in with subjects from
the life of Christ. A particularly splendid full-page
is that of the Virgin and Child under a Gothic
canopy, with gold diapered background. There are
also very interestingly designed genealogical trees,
and fine arrangements of double columned text-
pages with illuminated ornament (see Nos. 2, 3,
and 4, Appendix).

The Tenison Psalter (Addit. MS. 24686) is a
specimen of English thirteenth century work.
"Probably executed for Alphonso, son of Edmund I., on his contemplated marriage with
Margaret daughter of Florentius, Count of Holland, which was frustrated by the prince's death
on 1st August, 1224."

SPECULUM HUMANÆ VITÆ.   (AUGSBURG, GÜNTHER ZAINER, *circa* 1475.)

(*Size of original,* 6⅝ *in.* × 10⅕ *in.*)

The full-page miniatures arranged in panels—in some instances four on a page, with alternate burnished gold and dark blue diapered backgrounds behind the figures, and in others six on a page, the miniature much smaller, and set in a larger margin of colour, alternate red and blue—are very full, solid, and rich in colour with burnished gold. The book is further interesting, as giving excellent and characteristic instances of another and very different treatment of the page (and one which appears to have been rather peculiarly English in style), in the spiny scrolls which, often springing from a large illuminated initial letter upon the field of the text, spreads upon and down the margin, or above and below, often holding in its branching curves figures and animals, which in this MS. are beautifully and finely drawn. Note the one showing a lady of the time in pursuit of some deer.

In the thirteenth century books the text is a solid tower or column, from which excursions can be made by the fancy and invention of the designer, up and down and above and beneath, upon the ample vellum margins; in some cases, indeed, additional devices appear to have been added by other and later hands than those of the original scribe or illuminator.

There is a very remarkable Apocalypse (Brit. Mus. MSS. 17353; formerly belonging to the Carthusian house of Vau Dieu between Liege and Aix) by French artists of the early fourteenth century, which has a series of very fine imaginative and weird designs (suggestive of Orcagna), highly decorative in treatment, very full and frank in colour, and firm in outline. The designs are in oblong panels, inclosed in linear coloured borders at the head of each page, and occupying about two-thirds of it, the text being written in double columns beneath each miniature, with small illuminated initials. The backgrounds of the designs are diapered on grounds of dark green and red alternately.

The imaginative force and expression conveyed by these designs—strictly formal and figurative, and controlled by the ornamental traditions of the time—is very remarkable. The illustrator and decorator are here still one.

Queen Mary's Psalter (Brit. Mus. MS. Royal 2, B. VII.), again, is interesting as giving instances of a very different and lighter treatment of figure designs. We find in this MS., together with illuminations in full colours and burnished gold, a series of pale tinted illustrations in Bible history drawn with a delicate pen line.

The method of the illuminators and miniaturists seems always to have been to draw their figures and ornaments clearly out first with a pen before colouring.

In the full-coloured miniatures the pen lines are not visible, but in this MS. they are preserved with the delicate tinted treatment. The designs I speak of are placed two on a page, occupying it entirely. They are inclosed in vermilion borders, terminated at each corner with a leaf. There is a very distinct and graceful feeling about the designs. The same hand appears to have added on the lower margins of the succeeding text pages a series of quaint figures—combats of grotesque animals, hunting, hawking, and fishing scenes, and games

(COLOGNE, 1480.)

BIBLE, HEINRICH QUENTEL.

and sports, and, finally, Biblical subjects. Here, again, I think we may detect in the early illustrators a tendency to escape from the limitations of the book page, though only a tendency.

A fine ornamental page combining illumination with miniature is given in the "Epistle of Philippe de Comines to Richard II." at the end of the fourteenth century. The figures, interesting historically and as examples of costume, are relieved upon a diapered ground. The text is in double columns, with square initials, and the page is lightened by open foliation branching out upon the margin from the straight spiney border strips, which on the inner side terminate in a dragon.

As a specimen of early fifteenth century work, both for illuminator, scribe, and miniaturist, it would be difficult to find a more exquisite book than the Bedford Hours (Brit. Mus. MS. Add. 18850), dated 1422, said to be the work of French artists, though produced in England. The kalendar, which occupies the earlier pages, is remarkable for its small and very brilliant and purely coloured miniatures set like gems in a very fine, delicate, light, open, leafy border, bright with burnished gold trefoil leaves, which are characteristic of French illuminated books of this period (*see* Nos. 5 and 6, Appendix).

There is an elaborate full-page miniature containing the Creation and Fall, which breaks over the margin here and there. The thirteenth and fourteenth century miniaturists frequently allowed their designs to break over the framework of their diapered grounds or panels in an effective way, which pleasantly varied the formality of framed-in subjects upon the page, especially where a flat margin of colour between lines inclosed them; and some parts of the groups broke over the inner line while keeping within the limits of the outer one. Very frequently, as in this MS., a general plan is followed throughout in the spacing of the pages, though the borders and miniatures in detail show almost endless variation. In such splendid works as this we get the complete and harmonious co-operation and union between the illustrator and the decorator. The object of each is primarily to beautify his page. The illuminator makes his borders and initial letters branch and bud, and put forth leaves and flowers spreading luxuriantly up and down the margin of his vellum pages (beautiful even as the scribe left them) like a living growth; while the miniaturist makes the letter itself the shrine of some delicate saint, or a vision of some act of mercy or martyrdom; while the careless world plays hide and seek through the labyrinthine borders, as the seasons follow each other through the kalendar, and the peasant ploughs, and sows, and reaps, and threshes out the corn, while gay knights tourney in the lists, or, with ladies in their quaint attire, follow the spotted deer through the greenwood.

In these beautiful liturgical books of the Middle Ages, as we see, the ornamental feeling developed with and combined the illustrative function, so that almost any illuminated Psalter or Book of Hours will furnish not only lovely examples of floral decoration in borders and initials of endless fertility of invention, but also give us pictures of the life and manners of the times. In those of our own

country we can realize how full of colour, quaint
costume, and variety was life when England was

DUTCH SCHOOL.   XVTH CENTURY.

SPIEGEL ONSER BEHOUDENISSE, KUILENBURG. (JAN VELDENER, 1483.)

indeed merry, in spite of family feuds and tyran-
nous lords and kings; before her industrial transformation and the dispossession of her people; ere

Boards of Works and Poor-law Guardians took the place of her monasteries and abbeys; before her streams were fouled with sewage, and her cities blackened with coal smoke—the smoke of the burning sacrificed to commercial competition and wholesale production for profit by means of machine power and machine labour; before she became the workshop and engine-room of the world.

These books glowing with gold and colour tell of days when time was no object, and the pious artist and scribe could work quietly and lovingly to make a thing of beauty with no fear of a publisher or a printer before his eyes, or the demands of world market.

In the midst of our self-congratulation on the enormous increase of our resources for the rapid and cheap production of books, and the power of the printing press, we should do well not to forget that if books of those benighted centuries of which I have been speaking were few, comparatively, they were fit, though few—they were things of beauty and joys for ever to their possessors. A prayer-book was not only a prayer-book, but a picture-book, a shrine, a little mirror of the world, a sanctuary in a garden of flowers. One can well understand their preciousness apart from their religious use, and many have seen strange eventful histories no doubt. The Earl of Shrewsbury lost his prayer-book (the Talbot prayer-book) and his life together on the battle-field at Castillon (about thirty miles from Bordeaux) in 1453. This book, as Mr. Quaritch states, was carried away by a Breton soldier, and was only re-discovered in Brittany a few years ago.

Pithas   Thais   Cherea

"DEUTSCHE UEBERSETZUNG DES EUNUCHUS DES TERENTIUS."
(ULM, DINCKMUT, 1486.)

It has been suggested that the large coloured and illuminated initial letters in liturgical books had their origin as guides in taking up the different parts of the service; and, as I learn from Mr. Micklethwaite, in some of the Missals, where the crucifixion is painted in an illuminated letter, a simple cross is placed below for the votary to kiss instead of the picture, as it was found in practice, when only the picture was there, the tendency was to obliterate it by the recurrence of this form of devotion.

As an example of the influence of naturalism which had begun to make itself felt in art towards the end of the fifteenth century, we may cite The Romance of the Rose (Harl. MSS. 4425), in the British Museum, which has two fine full-page miniatures with elaborate borderings, full of detail and colour, and which are also illustrative of costume (*see* No. 8, Appendix). The text pages show the effect of double columns with small highly-finished miniatures (occupying the width of one column) interspersed. The style of work is akin to that of the celebrated Grimani Breviary, now in the library of St. Mark's, Venice, the miniatures of which are said to have been painted by Memling. They are wonderfully rich in detail, and fine in workmanship, and are quite in the manner of the Flemish pictures of that period. We feel that the pictorial and illustrative power is gaining the ascendancy, and in its borders of highly wrought leaves, flowers, fruit, and insects, given in full relief with their cast shadows—wonderful as they are in themselves as pieces of work—it is evident to me, at least, that whatever graphic strength and richness of chiaro-oscuro is gained it is at the distinct cost of the beauty of pure decorative effect upon the page. After the delicate arabesques of the earlier time, these borders look a little heavy, and however great their pictorial or imitative merits, they fail to satisfy the conditions of a page decoration so satisfactorily.

Perhaps the most sumptuous examples of book decoration of this period are to be found in Italy, in the celebrated Choir Books in the cathedral of Siena. They show a rare union of imaginative form, pictorial skill, and decorative sense in the miniaturist, united with all the Italian richness and grace in the treatment of early Renaissance ornament, and in its adaptation to the decoration of the book page (*see* No. 9, Appendix).

These miniatures are the work of Girolamo da Cremona, and Liberale da Verona. At least, these two are described as " the most copious and indefatigable of the artists employed on the Corali." Payments were made to them for the work in 1468, and again in 1472-3, which fixes the date.

I am not ignoring the possibility of a certain division of labour in the illuminated MS. The work of the scribe, the illuminator, and the miniaturist are distinct enough, while equally important to the result. Mr. J. W. Bradley, who has compiled a Dictionary of Miniaturists, speaking of calligrapher, illuminator, and miniaturist, says :— " Each of these occupations is at times conjoined with either or both of the others," and when that is so, in giving the craftsman his title, he decides by the period of his work. For instance, from the seventh to the tenth centuries he would call him

"LIFE OF CHRIST." (ANTWERP, GHERAERT LEEU, 1487.)

(*Original*, 7⅜ *in.* × 5⅛ *in.*)

calligrapher; eleventh to fifteenth centuries, illuminator; fifteenth to sixteenth centuries, miniaturist. Transcription he puts in another category as the work of the copyist scribe. But whatever division of labour there may or may not have been, there was no division in the harmony and unity of the effect. If in some cases the more purely ornamental parts, such as the floral borders and initials, were the work of one artist, the text of another, and the miniatures of another, all I can say is, that each worked together as brethren in unity, contributing to the beauty of a harmonious and organic whole; and if such division of labour can be ascertained to have been a fact, it goes to prove the importance of some co-operation in a work of art, and its magnificent possibilities.

The illuminated MS. books have this great distinction and advantage in respect of harmony of text and decoration, the text of the calligrapher always harmonizing with the designs of the illuminator, it being in like manner all through the Middle Ages a thing of growth and development, acquiring new characteristics and undergoing processes of transformation less obvious perhaps, but not less actual, than the changes in the style and characters of the devices and inventions which accompanied it. The mere fact that every part of the work was due to the hand, that manual skill and dexterity alone has produced the whole, gives a distinction and a character to these MS. books which no press could possibly rival.

The difficulty which besets the modern book decorator, illustrator, or designer of printers' ornaments, of getting type which will harmonize pro-

33　　　　　　　　　D

perly with his designs, did not exist with the mediæval illuminator, who must always have been sure of balancing his designs by a body of text not only beautiful in the form of its individual letters, but beautiful and rich in the effect of its mass on the page, which was only enhanced when the initials were relieved with colour on gold, or beautiful pen work which grew out of them like the mistletoe from the solid oak stem.

The very pitch of perfection which penmanship, or the art of the calligrapher had reached in the fifteenth century, the calculated regularity and "purgation of superfluities" in the form of the letters, the squareness of their mass in the words, and approximation in length and height, seem to suggest and naturally lead up to the idea of the movable type and the printed page.

Before, however, turning the next page of our subject, let us take one more general and rapid glance at the MS. books from the point of view of design.

While examples of the two fields into which art may be said to be always more or less divided— the imitative and the inventive, or the illustrative and the decorative—are not altogether absent in the books of the Middle Ages, the main tendency and prevailing spirit is decidedly on the inventive and decorative side, more especially in the work of the illuminators from the thirteenth to the fifteenth centuries, and yet this inventive and decorative spirit is often allied with a dramatic and poetic feeling, as well as a sense of humour. We see how full of life is the ornament of the illuminator, how figures, birds, animals, and insects fill his

"CHRONICA HUNGARIÆ."   (AUGSBURG, RATDOLT, 1488.)

arabesques, how he is often decorator, illustrator, and pictorial commentator in one.

Even apart from his enrichments, it is evident that the page was regarded by the calligrapher as

FRENCH SCHOOL.   XVᴛʜ CENTURY.

INITIAL FROM "LA MER DES HISTOIRES." (PARIS, PIERRE LE ROUGE, 1488.)

a space to be decorated—that it should at least, regarded solely as a page of text, be a page of beautiful writing, the mass carefully placed upon the vellum, so as to afford convenient and ample margin, especially beneath. The page of a book, in fact, may be regarded as a flat panel which may be variously spaced out. The calligrapher, the illuminator, and the miniaturist are the architects who planned out their vellum grounds and built beautiful structures of line and colour upon them for thought and fancy to dwell in. Sometimes the text is arranged in a single column, as generally in the earlier MSS.; sometimes in double, as generally in the Gothic and later MSS., and these square and oblong panels of close text are relieved by large and small initial letters sparkling in gold and colour, inclosed in their own framework, or escaping from it in free and varied branch work and foliation upon the margin, and set with miniatures like gems, as in the Bedford Hours, the larger initials increasing to such proportions as to inclose a more important miniature—a subject-picture in short—a book illustration in the fullest sense, yet strictly a part of a general scheme of the ornamentation of the page.

Floral borders, which in some instances spread freely around the text and fill the margins, unconfined though not uninfluenced by rectangular lines or limits from a light and open, yet rich and delicate tracery of leaves and fanciful blossoms (as in the Bedford Hours); are in others framed in with firm lines (Tenison Psalter, p. 11); and in later fifteenth century MSS. with gold lines and mouldings, as the treatment of the page becomes more pictorial and solid in colour and relief. Sometimes the borders form a distinct framework, inclosing the text and dividing its columns, as in "The Book of Hours of René of Anjou" (Egerton

"HORTUS SANITATIS."   (MAINZ, JACOB MEIDENBACH, 1491.)

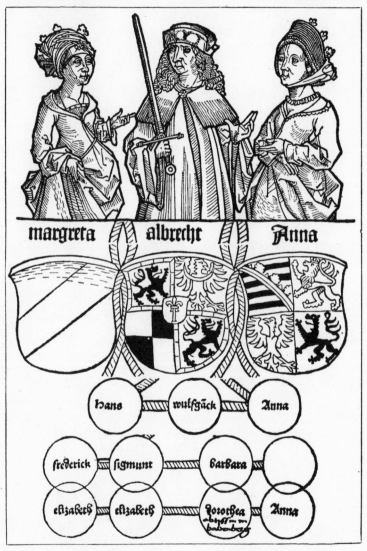

"CHRONEKEN DER SASSEN." (MAINZ, SCHÖFFER, 1492.)

MS. 1070), and the same design is sometimes repeated differently coloured. Gradually the miniaturist—the picture painter—although at first almost as formally decorative as the illuminator —asserts his independence, and influences the treatment of the border, which becomes a miniature also, as in the Grimani Breviary, the Romance of the Rose, and the Choir Books of Siena, until at last the miniature or the picture is in danger of being more thought of than the book, and we get books of framed pictures instead of pictured or decorated books. In the Grimani Breviary the miniature frequently occupies the whole page with a single subject-picture; or the miniature is superimposed upon a pictured border, which, strengthened by rigid architectural lines and tabernacle work, form a rich frame.

All these varieties we have been examining are, however, interesting and beautiful in their own way in their results. In considering any form of art of a period which shows active traditions, real life and movement, natural growth and development, we are fascinated by its organic quality, and though we may detect the absorption or adaptation of new elements and new influences from time to time leading to changes of style and structure of design, as well as changed temper and feeling, as long as this natural evolution continues, each variety has its own charm and its own compensations ; while we may have our preferences as to which approaches most nearly to the ideal of perfect adaptability, and, therefore, of decorative beauty.

In the progressive unfolding which characterizes

THE FIRST PERIOD.

a living style, all its stages must be interesting and possess their own significance, since all fall into their places in the great and golden record of the history of art itself.

CHAPTER II. OF THE TRANSITION, AND OF THE SECOND PERIOD OF DECORATIVELY ILLUSTRATED BOOKS, FROM THE INVENTION OF PRINTING IN THE FIFTEENTH CENTURY ONWARDS.

E have seen to what a pitch of perfection and magnificence the decoration and illustration of books attained during the Middle Ages, and the splendid results to which art in the three distinct forms— calligraphy, illumination, and miniature—contributed. We have traced a gradual progression and evolution of style through the period of MS. books, both in the development of writing and ornament. We have noted how the former became more and more regular and compact in its mass on the page, and how in the latter the illustrative or pictorial size grew more and more important, until at the close of the fifteenth century we had large and elaborately drawn and naturalistic pictures framed in the initial letters, as in the Choir Books of Siena, or occupying the whole page with a single subject, as in the Grimani Breviary. The tree of design, springing from small and obscure germs, sends up a strong stem, branches and buds in the favourable sun, and finally breaks into a beautiful free efflorescence and fruitage. Then we mark a fresh change. The autumn comes after the summertide, winter follows autumn, till the new life, ever ready to spring from the husk of the old, puts forth its leaves, until by almost imperceptible degrees and changes, and the silent growth of new forces, the face of the world is changed for us.

So it was with the change that came upon European art towards the end of the fifteenth century, the result of many causes working together; but as regards art as applied to books, the greatest of these was of course the invention and application of printing. Like most great movements in art or life, it had an obscure beginning. Its parentage might be sought in the woodcuts of the earlier part of the fifteenth century applied to the printing of cards. The immediate forerunners of printed books were the block books. Characteristic specimens of the quaint works may be seen displayed in the King's Library, British Museum. The art of these block books is quite rude and primitive, and, contrasted with the highly-finished work of the illuminated MS. of the same time, might almost belong to another period. These are the first tottering steps of the infant craft; the first faint utterances, soon to grow into strong, clear, and perfect speech, to rule the world of books and men.

Germany had not taken any especial or distinguished part in the production of MSS. remarkable for artistic beauty or original treatment; but her time was to come, and now, in the use of an artistic application of the invention of printing, and the new era of book decoration and illustration, she at once took the lead. Seeing that the invention itself is ascribed to one of her own sons, it seems appropriate enough, and natural that printing should grow to quick perfection in the

(LÜBECK, STEFFEN ARNDES, 1494.)

FROM THE LÜBECK BIBLE.

land of its birth; so that we find some of the earliest and greatest triumphs of the Press coming from German printers, such as Gutenberg, Fust, and Schœffer, not to speak yet of the wonderful fertility of decorative invention, graphic force, and dramatic power of German designers, culminating in the supreme genius of Albrecht Dürer and Hans Holbein.

The prosperous German towns, Cologne, Mainz, Frankfort, Strassburg, Augsburg, Bamberg, Halberstadt, Nuremberg, and Ulm, all became famous in the history of printing, and each had its school of designers in black and white, its distinctive style in book-decoration and printing.

Italy, France, Switzerland, and England, however, all had their share, and a glorious share, in the triumph of printing in its early days. The presses of Venice, of Florence, and of Rome and Naples, of Paris, and of Basel, and of our own William Caxton, at Westminster, must always be looked upon as in the van of the early progress of the art, and the richness of the decorative invention and beauty, in the case of the woodcut adornments used by the printers of Venice and Florence especially, gives them in the last years of the fifteenth century and the early years of the sixteenth a particular distinction.

1454 appears to be the earliest definite date that can be fixed on to mark the earliest use of printing. In that year, the Mainz "Indulgences" were in circulation, but the following year is more important, as to it is assigned the issue, from the press of Gutenberg and Fust at Mainz, of the famous Mazarin Bible, a copy of which is in the British

E

Museum. Mr. Bullen says, " The copy which first attracted notice in modern times was discovered in the library of Cardinal Mazarin "— hence the name.

It is noticeable as showing how transitional was the change in the treatment of the page. The scribe has been supplanted—the marshalled legions of printed letters have invaded his territory and driven him from his occupation ; but the margin is still left for the illuminator to spread his coloured borders upon, and the initial letters wait for the touch of colour from his hand. The early printers evidently regarded their art as providing a substitute for the MS. book. They aimed at doing the work of the scribe and doing it better and more expeditiously. No idea of a new departure in effect seems to have been entertained at first, to judge from such specimens as these.

Another early printed book is the Mainz Psalter. It is printed on vellum, and comes from the press of Fust and Schœffer in 1457. It is remarkable not only as the first printed psalter and as the first book printed with a date, but also as being the first example of printing in colours. The initial letter B is the result of this method, and it affords a wonderful instance of true register. The blue of the letter fitted cleanly into the red of the surrounding ornament with a precision which puzzles our modern printers, and it is difficult to understand how such perfection could have been attained. Mr. Emery Walker has suggested to me that the blue letter itself might have been cut out, inked, and dropped in from the back of the red block when that was in the press, and so the two colours printed together. If this could be done with sufficient precision, it would certainly account for the exactitude of the register. Apart from this interesting technical question, however, the page

FRENCH SCHOOL. XVTH CENTURY.

FROM PARIS ET VIENNE. (PARIS, JEHAN TREPEREL, C. 1495.)

is a very beautiful one, and the initial, with its solid shape of figured blue, inclosed in the delicate red pen-like tracery climbing up and down the margin, is a charming piece of page decoration. The original may be seen in one of the cases in the King's Library, British Museum. We have here an instance of the printer aiming at directly imitating and supplanting by his craft the art of the calligrapher and illuminator, and with such a beauty and perfection of workmanship as must have astonished them and given them far more reason to regard the printer as a dangerous rival than had (as it is said) the early wood engravers, who were unwilling to help the printer by their art for fear his craft would injure their own, which seems somewhat extraordinary considering how closely allied both wood engraver and printer have been ever since. The example of the Mainz Psalter does not seem to have been much followed, and as regards the application of colour, it was as a rule left as a matter of course to be added by the miniaturist, who evidently declined as an artist after he had got into the way of having his designs in outline provided for him ready-made by the printer; or, rather, perhaps the accomplished miniature printer, having carried his art as applied to books about as far as it would go, became absorbed as a painter of independent pictures, and the printing of books fell into inferior hands. There can be no doubt that the devices and decorations of the early printers were intended to be coloured in emulation of illuminated and miniatured MSS., and were regarded, in fact, as the pen outlines of the illuminator, only complete when filled in with colours and gold. It appears to have been only by degrees that the rich and vigorous lines of the woodcut, as well as the black and white effect, became admired for their own sake—so slowly moves the world!

A good idea of the general character of the development of the wood (and metal) cut in book and illustration and decoration in Germany, from

Die viij. fabel von den hafen vnd fröfchen.

DAS BUCH UND LEBEN DES HOCHBERÜHMTEN FABELDICHTERS ÆSOPI."
(ULM, 1498.[1])

1470 (Leiden Christi, Pfister, Bamberg, 1470) to (Virgil Solis' Bible) 1563, may be gained from a study of the series of reproductions given in this

---

[1] This is the date of the copy from which the illustration is reproduced. The first edition of the book was, however, probably issued about 1480.

OF THE TRANSITION.

and the preceding chapter, in chronological order, with the names, dates, and places, as well as the particular characteristics of the style of the different designers and printers.

The same may be said in regard to the Italian series which follows, and those from Basel and Paris.

ITALIAN SCHOOL.   XVTH CENTURY.

DE CLARIS MULIERIBUS.   (FERRARA, 1497.)

Perhaps the most interesting examples of the use of early printing as a substitute for illumination and miniature are to be found in the Books of Hours which were produced at Paris in the later years of the fifteenth and the early years of the sixteenth centuries (1487-1519 about) by Vérard, Du Pré, Philip Pigouchet, Kerver, and Hardouyn.

Specimens of these books may be seen in the British Museum, and at the Art Library at South Kensington Museum. The originals are mostly printed on vellum.

The effect of the richly designed borders on

54

black dotted grounds is very pleasant, but these
books seem to have been intended to be illumi-

ITALIAN SCHOOL.   XVᴛʜ CENTURY.

TUPPO'S ÆSOP.   (NAPLES, 1485.)

nated and coloured.   We find in some copies that
the full-page printed pictures are coloured, being

worked up as miniatures, and the semi-architectural borderings with Renaissance mouldings and details are gilded flat, and treated as the frame of the picture. There is one which has the mark of

ITALIAN SCHOOL. XVTH CENTURY.

P. CREMONESE'S "DANTE." (VENICE, NOVEMBER, 1491.)

the printer Gillet Hardouyn (G. H. on the shield), on the front page. In another copy (1515) this is painted and the framework gilded; the subject is Nessus the Centaur carrying off Deianira, the wife

56

of Hercules; a sign of the tendency to revive
classical mythology which had set in, in this case,
in curious association with a Christian service-
book. It is noticeable how soon the facility for

ITALIAN SCHOOL.   XVᴛʜ CENTURY.

THE DISCOVERY OF THE INDIES.   (FLORENCE, 1493.)

repetition by the press was taken advantage of,
and a design, especially if on ornamental borderings
of a page, often repeated several times throughout
a book. These borderings and ornaments being

generally in separate blocks as to headings, side panels, and tail-pieces, could easily be shifted and a certain variety obtained by being differently made up. Here we may see commercialism creeping in. Considerations of profit and economy no doubt have their effect, and mechanical invention

ITALIAN SCHOOL. XVᴛʜ CENTURY.

FIOR DI VIRTÙ. 1498·(FLORENCE, 1493?)

comes in to cheapen not only labour, but artistic invention also.

It took some time, however, to turn the printer into the manufacturer or tradesman pure and simple. Nothing is more striking than the high artistic character of the early printed books. The invention of printing, coming as it did when the illuminated MSS. had reached the period of its greatest glory and perfection, with the artistic

STEPHANO CAESENATE PEREGRINI INVENTORE (S.C. P.I.). (VENICE, DE GREGORIIS, 1498.)

traditions of fifteen centuries poured, as it were, into its lap, filling its founts with beautiful letter-ing, and guiding the pencil of its designers with a still unbroken sense of fitness and perfect adap-tability ; while as yet the influence of the revival of classic learning and mythology was only felt as the stirring and stimulating breath of new awakening spring—the aroma of spice-laden winds from un-known shores of romance—or as the mystery and wonder of discovery, standing on the brink of a half-disclosed new world, and fired with the thought of its possibilities—

> "Or like stout Cortez when with eagle eyes
> He stared at the Pacific."

Had the discovery of printing occurred two or three centuries earlier, it would have been curious to see the results. But after all, an invention never lives until the world is ready to adopt it. It is impossible to say how many inventions are new inventions. "Ask and ye shall have," or the practical application of it, is the history of civiliza-tion. Necessity, the stern mother, compels her children to provide for their own physical and in-tellectual necessities, and in due time the hour and the man (with his invention) arrives.

Classical mythology and Gothic mysticism and romance met together in the art and books of the early Renaissance. Ascetic aspiration strives with frank paganism and nature worship. The gods of ancient Greece and Rome seemed to awake after an enchanted sleep of ages, and reappear again unto men.

Italy, having hardly herself ever broken with

the ancient traditions of Classical art and religion, became the focus of the new light, and her independent republics, such as Florence and Venice, the centres of wealth, culture, refinement, and artistic invention. Turkish conquest, too, had its effect on the development of the new movement by driving Greek scholars and the knowledge of the classical writers of antiquity Westward. These were all materials for an exceptional development of art, and, above all, of the art of the printer, and the decoration and illustration of books.

The name of Aldus, of Venice, is famous among those of the early Renaissance printers. Perhaps the most remarkable book, from this or any press, for the beauty of its decorative illustration, is the *Poliphili Hypnerotomachia*—" The Dream of Poliphilus"—printed in 1499, an allegorical romance of love in the manner of those days. The authorship of the design has been the subject of much speculation. I believe they were attributed at one time to Mantegna, and they have also been ascribed to one of the Bellini. The style of the designer, the quality of the outline, the simplicity yet richness of the designs, their poetic feeling, the mysticism of some, and frank paganism of others, places the series quite by themselves. The first edition is now very difficult to obtain, and might cost something like 100 guineas.

My illustrations are taken from the copy in the Art Library at South Kensington Museum, and are from negatives taken by Mr. Griggs, for the Science and Art Department, who have issued a set of reproductions in photo-lithography, by him, of the whole of the woodcuts in the volume,

ITALIAN SCHOOL.

POLIPHILUS.

EL QVARTO triũpho q̃tro rote el portauão di ferrineo Aſueſto

(VENICE, ALDUS, 1499.)

TERTIVS

(VENICE, ALDUS, 1499.)

POLIPHILUS.

65 F

ALESSANDRO MINUZIANO.   (MILAN, DESIGNER UNKNOWN, 1503.)

SCHOOL OF GIOV. BELLINI.

(VENICE, GEORGIUS DE RUSCONIBUS, 1506.)

THE DESCENT OF MINERVA, FROM THE QUATRIREGIO.

(FLORENCE, 1508)

AULUS GELLIUS, PRINTED BY GIOV. TACUINO.   (VENICE, 1509.)

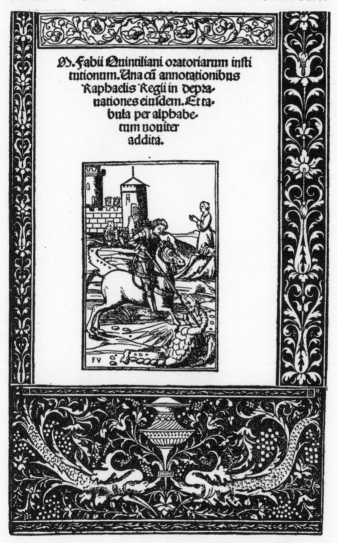

M. Fabii Quintiliani oratoriarum insti
tutionum. Una cū annotationibus
Raphaelis Regii in deprauationes eiusdem. Et tabula per alphabetum nouiter
addita.

QUINTILIAN.   (VENICE, GEORGIUS DE RUSCONIBUS, 1512.)

75

❡ Secūda pars operis dñicæ paſſionis & reſurrectionis diē i dagat, & iudæorꝫ ſup hoc argumēta confutat.

Tſi multa ſunt argumenta, quibus iudæi magnãm no bis calumniã ſolent aſtrue re, & fidem ſperatæ a nobis reſurrectionis ſtulta garrulitate deridere, in hac tamē lucubratiuncula ·noſtra ea duntaxat confutare aggrediemur, quæ dominicæ paſsionis & reſurrectionis materiam concernunt. Solet nanꝙ obſtinatum illud, & ſeruile iudæorum pecus in Chriſti ſaluatoris blaſphemiam exire propenſius & in chriſtianorum calumniam inſultare audentius & confidentius, quia legis noſtræ munimenta non pauca ex auita ipſorum religione mutuati ſumus ea præcipue, quæ agni paſchalis typo, domini paſſionem ſignificabant: quo fit ut perperam interpretan tes legem, & diuini ſacra menti myſterium contami nantes, multas indies calumnias nobis inferre nõ deſiſtant, nunquam cauillandi finem facientes: adeo ꝙ cõtinuis ſubſãnationibus nos laceſſentes, & ſingulas obſeruationes noſtras deteſtãtes perpetuis ipſoꝫ cõtumeliis, atꝙ conuitiis ſimus obnoxii: non ſolum in paſchæ celebratione obſeruationē noſtram ludibrio maximoꝙ opprobrio ducentes (de quo ſuperiori lu cubratiuncula noſtra ſcripſimus) uerũ etiam i dñicæ paſſionis myſterio ruditatis, & iſcitiæ nos iſimulãtes

A. ii

OTTAVIANO DEI PETRUCCI.　　　(FOSSOMBRONE, 1513.)

of the original size, at the price, I believe, of
5s. 6d. Here is an instance of what photographic
reproduction can do for us — when originals
of great works are costly or unattainable we can
get reproductions for a few shillings, for all practical purposes as good for study as the originals
themselves. If we cannot, in this age, produce
great originals, we can at least reproduce them—
perhaps the next best thing.

There is a French edition of Poliphilus printed
at Paris, by Kerver, in 1561,[1] which has a frontispiece designed by Jean Cousin. The illustrations,
too, have all been redrawn, and are treated in
quite a different manner from the Venetian
originals—but they have a character of their
own, though of a later, florid, and more self-
conscious type, as might be expected from Paris
in the latter half of the sixteenth century. The
initial letters of a series of chapters in the book
spell, if read consecutively, Francisco Columna
(F.R.A.N.C.I.S.C.O.   C.O.L.V.M.N.A.) — the
name of the writer of the romance.

Whether such designs as these were intended
to be coloured is doubtful. They are very satisfactory as they are in outline, and want nothing
else. The book may be considered as an illustrated one, drawings of monuments, fountains,
standards, emblems, and devices are placed here
and there in the text, but they are so charmingly
designed and drawn that the effect is decorative,
and being in open line the mechanical conditions
are perfectly fulfilled of surface printing with the
type.

[1] The first French edition is dated 1546.

OF THE TRANSITION.

After the beautiful productions of the German, Italian (of which some reproductions are given here), and French printers, our own William Caxton's first books seem rather rough, though not without character, and, at any rate, picturesqueness, if they cannot be quoted as very accomplished examples of the printer's art. The first book printed in England is said to be Caxton's " Dictes and Sayings of the Philosophers," printed by him at Westminster in 1477.

A noticeable characteristic of the early printed books is the development of the title page. Whereas the MSS. generally did without one, with the advent of printing the title page became more and more important, and even if there were no other illustrations or ornaments in a book, there was often a woodcut title. Such examples as some here given convey a good idea of what charming decorative feeling these title page designs sometimes displayed, and those greatest of designers and book decorators and illustrators, Albrecht Dürer and Hans Holbein, showed their power and decorative skill, and sense of the resources of the woodcut, in the designs made by them for various title pages.

The noble designs of the master craftsman of Nuremberg, Albrecht Dürer, are well known. His extraordinary vigour of drawing, and sense of its resources as applied to the woodcut, made him a great force in the decoration and illustration of books, and many are the splendid designs from his hand. Three designs from the fine series of the Little Passion and two of his title pages are given, which show him on the strictly decorative

ALBRECHT DÜRER, "KLEINE PASSION."   (NUREMBERG, 1512.)

ALBRECHT DÜRER, "KLEINE PASSION."   (NUREMBERG, 1512.)

ALBRECHT DÜRER, "KLEINE PASSION."   (NUREMBERG, 1512.)

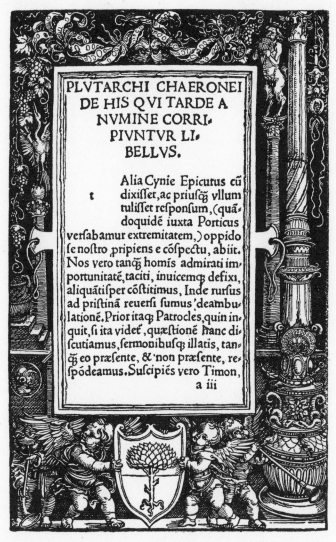

PLVTARCHI CHAERONEI
DE HIS QVI TARDE A
NVMINE CORRI‧
PIVNTVR LI‧
BELLVS.

Alia Cynie Epicurus cū
dixiſſet, ac priuſᖇ vllum
tuliſſet reſponſum, (quā‧
doquidē iuxta Porticus
verſabamur extremitatem,) oppido
ſe noſtro pripiens e cōſpectu, abiit.
Nos vero tanᖇ homis admirati im‧
portunitatē, taciti, inuicemᖅ defixi,
aliquātiſper cōſtitimus, Inde rurſus
ad priſtinā reuerſi ſumus 'deambu‧
latione. Prior itaᖅ Patrocles, quin in‧
quit, ſi ita videt, quæſtionē hanc di‧
ſcutiamus, ſermonibuſᖅ illatis, tan‧
ᖇ eo præſente, & 'non præſente, re‧
ſpōdeamus. Suſcipiēs vero Timon,
a iii

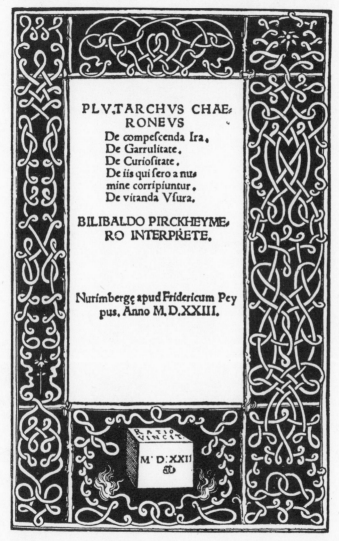

PLV.TARCHVS CHAE=
RONEVS
De compefcenda Ira.
De Garrulitate.
De Curiofitate.
De iis qui fero a nu=
mine corripiuntur.
De vitanda Vfura.

BILIBALDO PIRCKHEYME=
RO INTERPRETE.

Nurimbergę apud Fridericum Pey
pus. Anno M.D.XXIII.

RATIO
VINCIT
M·D·XXII

DESIGNED BY ALBRECHT DÜRER.   (NUREMBERG, 1523.)

side. The title dated 1523 may be compared
with that of Oronce Finé (Paris, 1534). There
appears to have been a return to this convoluted
knotted kind of ornament at this period. It
appears in Italian MSS. earlier, and may have
been derived from Byzantine sources.

There is a fine
title page designed
by Holbein, printed
by Petri, at Basle, in
1524. It was ori-
ginally designed and
used for an edition
of the New Testa-
ment, printed by the
same Adam Petri in
1523. At the four
corners are the sym-
bols of the Evangel-
ists; the arms of the
city of Basle are in
the centre of the
upper border, and
the printer's device
occupies a corre-
sponding space
below. Figures of

GER. SCHOOL. XVITH CENT.

HOLBEIN. "DANCE OF DEATH."
THE NUN. (LYONS, 1538.)

SS. Peter and Paul are in the niches at each side.
But the work always most associated with the
name of Holbein is the remarkable little book containing the series of designs known as the " Dance
of Death," the first edition of which was printed at
Lyons in 1538. The two designs here given are
printed from the blocks cut by Bonner and Byfield

HANS HOLBEIN:
(1833). These cuts are only about $2\frac{1}{2}$ by 2 inches, and yet an extraordinary amount of invention, graphic power, dramatic and tragic force, and grim and satiric humour, is compressed into them. They stand quite alone in the history of art, and give a wonderfully interesting and complete series of illustrations of the life of the sixteenth century. Holbein is supposed to have painted this "Dance of Death" in the palace of Henry VIII., erected by Cardinal Wolsey at Whitehall, life size ; but this was destroyed in the fire which consumed nearly the whole of that palace in 1697.

The Bible cuts of Hans Holbein are also a very fine series, and remarkable for their breadth and simplicity of line, as well as decorative effect on the page.

It is interesting to note that Holbein's father and grandfather both practised engraving and painting at Augsburg, while his brother Ambrose was also a fertile book illustrator. Hans Holbein the elder married a daughter of the elder Burgmair, father of the famous Hans Burgmair, examples of

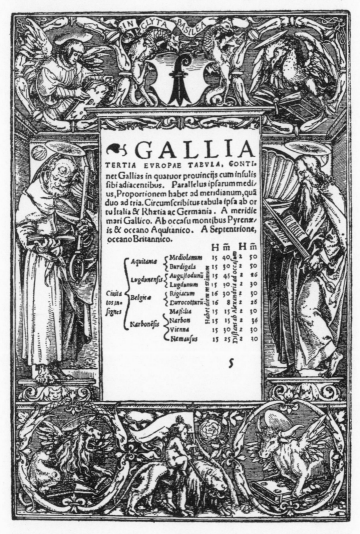

IN CLYTA BASILEA

GALLIA

TERTIA EVROPAE TABVLA, CONTI-
net Gallias in quatuor prouincijs cum insulis
sibi adiacentibus. Parallelus ipsarum medi-
us, Proportionem habet ad meridianum, quã
duo ad tria. Circumscribitur tabula ipsa ab or
tu Italia & Rhætia ac Germania. A meridie
mari Gallico. Ab occasu montibus Pyrenæ-
is & oceano Aquitanico. A Septentrione,
oceano Britannico.

			H m̃		H m̃	
Ciuita tos in- signes	Aquitanæ	Mediolanum	15	40	2	50
		Burdigala	15	50	2	50
	Lugdunensis	Augustodunũ	15	45	2	26
		Lugdunum	15	50	2	30
	Belgicæ	Rigiacum	16	30	2	50
		Durocottorũ	16	8	2	26
	Narbonēsis	Massilia	15	15	2	50
		Narbon	15	15	2	36
		Vienna	15	50	2	50
		Nemausus	15	25	2	30

Habet diem meridiem

Distans ab Alexandria ad occasum

5

HANS HOLBEIN.   (BASEL, ADAM PETRI, *circa* 1524.)

93

whose fine and vigorous style of drawing are given.

Albrecht Dürer and Holbein, indeed, seem to express and to sum up all the vigour and power of design of that very vigorous and fruitful time of the German Renaissance. They had able

GERMAN SCHOOL. XVITH CENTURY.

HANS HOLBEIN. HIST. VET. TEST. ICONIBUS ILLUSTRATA.

contemporaries, of course, among whom are distinguished, Lucas Cranach (the elder) born 1470, and Hans Burgmair, already named, who was associated with Dürer in the work of the celebrated series of woodcuts, "The Triumphs of Maximilian;" one of the fine series of "Der Weiss König," a noble title page, and a vigorous drawing of peasants at work in a field, here represent him. Other notable designers were

95

Hans Sebald Beham, Hans Baldung Grün, Hans Wächtlin, Jost Amman, and others, who carried on the German style or tradition in design to the end of the sixteenth century. This tradition of convention was technically really the mode of expression best fitted to the conditions of the woodcut

GERMAN SCHOOL. XVITH CENTURY.

HANS HOLBEIN. HIST. VET. TEST. ICONIBUS ILLUSTRATA.

and the press, under which were evolved the vigorous pen line characteristic of the German masters. It was a living condition in which each could work freely, bringing in his own fresh observation and individual feeling, while remaining in collective harmony.

The various marks adopted by the printers themselves are often decorative devices of great interest and beauty. The French printers, Gillett

AMBROSE HOLBEIN.   "DAS GANTZE NEUE TESTAMENT," ETC.

(BASEL, 1523.)

HANS BURGMAIR. "DER WEISS KÖNIG" (1512-14).

HANS BURGMAIR.

IOI

(AUGSBURG, 1516.)

HANS BURGMAIR. "HISTORIA MUNDI NATURALIS," PLINY. (FRANKFORT, 1582.)

HANS BURGMAIR. "DIE MEERFAHRT ZU VILN ONERKANNTEN INSELN UND KUNIGREICHEN."

(AUGSBURG, 1509.)

Hardouyn and Thielman Kerver, for instance, had charming devices with which they generally occupied the front page of their Books of Hours.

mortuoꝝ. ℣. Cecū ꝓncipiū in die virtuꝭ tue. Jn ſplēdoribꝮ ſctōꝝ eꞇ ꞇc. Oratio. DEus q̄ nobis nati ſaluatorꝭ die ꝯce dis celebꝛare octauū:fac nos q̄s ei⁹ ꝑpetua diuinitate muniri: cui⁹ ſum⁹ carnali cōmertio repati. Qui cū deo paꞇ tre ꞇ ſpiritu ſancto viuis ꞇ regnas ꞇc.

Jn die epipbanie domini.

OribꝮ miracuꞇ lis ozna tum diē ſancrum colimꝰ bodie ſtella ma gos duꞇ rit ad ꝑꞇ ſepium. bodie vi num eꞇ aqua faꞇ ctū ē ad p viꞇ

HANS BALDUNG GRÜN.   "HORTULUS ANIMÆ."

(STRASSBURG, MARTIN FLACH, 1511.)

Others were pictorial puns and embodied the name of the printer under some figure, such as that of Petri of Basle, who adopted a device of a stone, which the flames and the hammer stroke failed to destroy; or the mark of Philip le Noir—a black shield with a negro crest and supporter;

Ꝯalue
dies san
ctitatis/
leticie et
felicita/
tis: q̃ es
celsior cũ
ctis san
ctis; san
ctior oĩ/
bus: dul
cior vni
uersis.
Salue
dies mi
sericor/
die ꞇ li/

berationis: que es viuis gaudium ꞇ de/
functis refrigeriũ. Salue dies preclara:
angelis ꞇ hoĩbᵹ chara: in qua nos jesus
redemit: ꞇ planctũ nostrũ in gaudiũ con
uertit. Salue dies festa: in q̃ cõsolantur
corda mesta. Salue glia dierũ: in q̃ oĩs
ĩ paradisum restituit hoĩeᵹ reũ. Ꝑer istiꝰ
drei sacratissimi merita gliosaꞇ ꞇ ꝑ tuã le
q̃ ꝯ̃

or the palm tree of Palma Isingrin. Others were purely emblematic and heraldic, such as the dolphin twined round the anchor, of Aldus, with

the motto *"Propera tarde"*—" hasten slowly."
This, and another device of a crab holding a
butterfly by its wings, with the same signification,
are both borrowed from the favourite devices of
two of the early emperors of Rome—Augustus
and Titus. This
symbolic, emblem-
atic, allegorizing ten-
dency which had
been more or less
characteristic of both
art and literature, in
various degrees, from
the most ancient
times, became more
systematically culti-
vated, and collections
of emblems began
to appear in book
form in the sixteenth
century. The earliest
being that of Alciati,
the first edition of
whose book appeared
in 1522, edition after
edition following

HANS BALDUNG GRÜN.

" HORTULUS ANIMÆ."

(STRASSBURG, 1510-11.)

each other from various printers and places from
that date to 1621, with ever-increasing additions,
and being translated into French, German, and
Italian. Mr. Henry Green, the author of
" Shakespeare and the Emblem Writers " (written
to prove Shakespeare's acquaintance with the
emblem books, and constant allusions to emblems),
said of Alciati's book that " it established, if it

did not introduce, a new style for emblem literature
—the classical, in the place of the simply grotesque
and humorous, or of the heraldic and mystic."

There is an edition of Alciati printed at Lyons
(Bonhomme), 1551, a reprint of which was published by the Hol-
bein Society in 1881.
The figure designs
and the square wood-
cut subjects are sup-
posed to be the work
of Solomon Bernard
—called the little Ber-
nard—born at Lyons
in 1522. These are
surrounded by elabo-
rate and rather heavy
decorative borders, in
the style of the later
Renaissance, by an-
other hand, some of
them bearing the
monogram P.V.,
which has been ex-
plained to mean either
Pierino del Vaga, the
painter (a pupil of Raphael's), or Petro de
Vingles, a printer of Lyons.

HANS BALDUNG GRÜN.

"HORTULUS ANIMÆ."

(STRASSBURG, 1510-11.)

These borders, as we learn from a preface to
one of the editions ("Ad Lectorem"—Roville's
Latin text of the emblems), were intended as
patterns for various craftsmen. "For I say this
is their use, that as often as any one may wish to
assign fulness to empty things, ornament to base

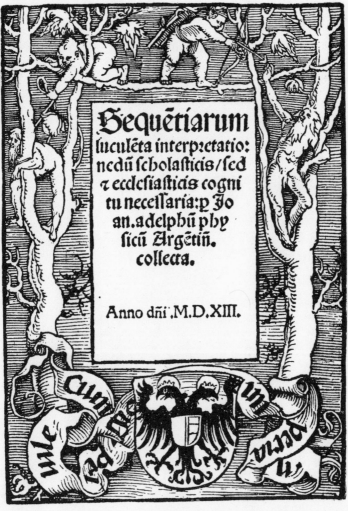

Bequētiarum
luculēta interpꝛetatio:
nedū ſcholaſticis / ſed
ꝛ eccleſiaſticis cogni
tu neceſſaria:ꝑ Jo
an.adelphū phy
ſicū Argētiñ.
collecta.

Anno dñi .M.D.XIII.

HANS WÄCHTLIN.   (STRASSBURG, MATHIAS SCHÜRER, 1513.)

III

HANS SEBALD BEHAM. "DAS PAPSTTHUM MIT SEINEN GLIEDERN."
(NUREMBERG, HANS WANDEREISEN, 1526.)

things, speech to dumb things, and reason to
senseless things, he may, from a little book of
emblems, as from an excellently well-prepared
hand-book, have what he may be able to impress
on the walls of houses, on windows of glass, on
tapestry, on hangings, on tablets, vases, ensigns,
seals, garments, the table, the couch, the arms,
the sword, and lastly, furniture of every kind."

An emblem has been defined (" Cotgrave's
Dictionary," Art. " Emblema ") as "a picture and
short posie, expressing some particular conceit;"
and by Francis Quarles as "but a silent parable;"
and Bacon, in his "Advancement of Learning,"
says :—" Embleme deduceth conceptions intellec-
tuall to images sensible, and that which is sensible
more fully strikes the memory, and is more easily
imprinted than that which is intellectual."

All was fish that fell into the net of the emblem
writer or deviser; hieroglyphic, heraldry, fable,
mythology, the ancient Egyptians, Homer, ancient
Greece and Rome, Christianity, or pagan philosophy, all in their turn served

"To point a moral and adorn a tale."

As to the artistic quality of the designs which are
found in these books, they are of very various
quality, those of the earlier sixteenth century with
woodcuts being naturally the best and most
vigorous, corresponding in character to the qualities of the contemporary design. Holbein's
"Dance of Death," or rather "Images and Storied
Aspects of Death," its true title, might be called
an emblem book, but very few can approach it in

artistic quality. Some of the devices in early editions of the emblem books of Giovio, Witney, and even the much later Quarles have a certain quaintness; but though such books necessarily depended on their illustrations, the moral and philosophic, or epigrammatic burden proved in the end more than the design could carry, when the impulse which characterized the early Renaissance had declined, and design, as applied to books, became smothered with classical affectation and pomposity, and the clear and vigorous wood-cut was supplanted by the doubtful advantage of the copper-plate. The introduction of the use of the copper-plate marks a new era in book illus-tration, but as regards their decoration, one of distinct decline. While the surface-printed block, whether woodcut or metal engraving (by which method many of the early book illustrations were rendered) accorded well with the conditions of the letter-press printing, as they were set up with the type and printed by the same pressure in the same press. With copper-plate quite other conditions came in, as the paper has to be pressed into the etched or engraved lines of the plate, instead of being impressed by the lines in relief of the wood or the metal. Thus, with the use of copper-plate illustrations in printed books, that mechanical relation which exists between a surface-printed block and the letter-press was at once broken, as a different method of printing had to be used. The apparent, but often specious, refinement of the copper-plate did not necessarily mean extra power or refinement of draughtsmanship or design, but merely thinner lines, and these were often

REFORMATION DER BAŸRISCHEN LANDRECHT.   (MUNICH, 1518.)

attained at the cost of richness and vigour, as well as decorative effect.

The first book illustrated with copper-plate engravings, however, bears an early date—1477. ["El Monte Sancto di Dio." Niccolo di Lorenzo, Florence]. In this case it was reserved for the full page pictures. The method does not seem to have commended itself much to the book designers, and did not come into general use until the end of the sixteenth century, with the decline of design.

The encyclopædic books of this period—the curious compendiums of the knowledge of those days — were full of entertaining woodcuts, diagrams, and devices, and the various treatises on grammar, arithmetic, geometry, physiology, anatomy, astronomy, geography, were made attractive by them, each section preceded perhaps by an allegorical figure of the art or science discoursed of in the costume of a grand dame of the period. The herbals and treatises on animals were often filled with fine floral designs and vigorous, if sometimes half-mythical, representations of animals.

There are fine examples of plant drawing in a beautiful herbal ("Fuchsius: De Historia Stirpium"; Basle, Isingrin, 1542). They are not only faithful and characteristic as drawings of the plants themselves, but are beautiful as decorative designs, being drawn in a fine free style, and with a delicate sense of line, and well thrown upon the page. At the beginning of the book is a woodcut portrait of the author, Leonard Fusch—possibly the fuschia may have been named after him—and at the end is another woodcut giving the portrait of the artist, the designer of the flowers, and the draughtsman on wood and the formschneider, or engraver on wood, beneath, who appears to be fully conscious of his own importance. The first two are busy at work, and it will be noticed the artist is drawing from the flower itself with the point of a brush, the brush being fixed in a quill in the manner of our water-colour brushes. The draughtsman holds the design or paper while he copies it upon the block. The portraits are vigorously drawn in a style suggestive of Hans Burgmair. Good examples of plant drawing which is united with design are also to be found in Matthiolus (Venice, 1583), and in a Kreuterbuch (Strasburg, 1551), and in Gerard's Herbal, of which there are several editions.

As examples of design in animals, there are some vigorous woodcuts in a "History of Quadrupeds," by Conrad Gesner, printed by Froschover, of Zurich, in 1554. The porcupine is as like a porcupine as need be, and there can be no mistake about his quills. The drawings of birds are excellent, and one of a crane (as I ought, perhaps, more particularly to know) is very characteristic.

But we have passed the Rubicon—the middle of the sixteenth century. Ripening so rapidly, and blossoming into such excellence and perfection as did the art of the printer, and design as applied to the printed page, through the woodcut and the press, their artistic character and beauty was somewhat short-lived. Up to about this date (1554 was the date of our last example), as we have seen, to judge only from the comparatively few specimens given here, what beautiful books were

Ambro
sius Calepinus
bergomates pro
fessor deuotissimus ordinis Eremitarum
sancti Augustini: Dictionum latinarum: τ
graecarum iterpres perspicacissimus: om
niumque Cornucopiae vocabulorum iser
tor sagacissimus: ita: vt in vnum coegerit
volumen Nonium Marcellum: Heitum
Pompeium: Marcum Varronem: δ er
uti: Donatum: Vallensemque: τ δ uidae
plurimum argiuo functus officio: litera
rraque palestra.

CALEPINVS AD LIBRVM.

Mos est putidus, & nouus repertus,   Nullis mobile veritas, fidei'q, est
Ingens materia vt queat videri,   His demptus liber exeat aperta
Predarus'q, liber, bonus'q totas,   In vulgus facie, fauore nullo,
Versus addere nominit probati,   Et graiis galeatus, & latinis :
Mentiris titulis, rubore nulle,   Nam (credas) alii magis, q ipse,
Obscuri'q viri, radiis'q vatis,   Querent auxilium , peras ab illis :
Auctor sic quasi nunc, bonus'q, fiat,   Sed si flatus olet, proba, legas'q,

IACOBVS FELICIANVS REGAZOLA,
STVDIOSIS.

Horrida Parnasi scopulis iuga quisquis adire,
Quisquis & Aonidum florida rura cupis.
Musarum cupidis concessus munere Diuum
Et Calepinus adest, hoc duce carpe viam.

PICTORES OPERIS,

Heinricus Füllmaurer.   Albertus Meyer.

SCVLPTOR
Vitus Rodolph. Speckle.

"FUCHSIUS: DE HISTORIA STIRPIUM."   (BASLE, ISINGRIN, 1542.)

printed, remarkable both for their decorative and illustrative value, and often uniting these two functions in perfect harmony; but after the middle of the sixteenth century both vigour and beauty in design generally may be said to have declined. Whether the world had begun to be interested in other things—and we know the great discovery of Columbus had made it practically larger—whether discovery, conquest, and commerce more and more filled the view of foremost spirits, and art was only valued as it illustrated or contributed to the knowledge of or furtherance of these; whether the Reformation or the spirit of Protestantism, turning men's minds from outward to inward things, and in its revolt against the half paganized Catholic Church—involving a certain ascetic scorn and contempt for any form of art which did not serve a direct moral purpose, and which appealed to the senses rather than to the emotions or the intellect —practically discouraged it altogether. Whether that new impulse given to the imagination by the influence of the revival of Classical learning, poetry, and antique art, had become jaded, and, while breaking with the traditions and spirit of Gothic or Mediæval art, began to put on the fetters of authority and pedantry, and so, gradually overlaid by the forms and cerements of a dead style, lost its vigour and vitality—whether due to one or all of these causes, certain it is that the lamp of design began to fail, and, compared with its earlier radiance, shed but a doubtful flicker upon the page through the succeeding centuries.

CHAPTER III. OF THE PERIOD OF THE DECLINE OF DECORATIVE FEELING IN BOOK DESIGN AFTER THE SIXTEENTH CENTURY, AND OF THE MODERN REVIVAL.

AS I indicated at the outset of the first chapter, my purpose is not to give a complete historical account of the decoration and illustration of books, but rather to dwell on the artistic treatment of the page from my own point of view as a designer. So far, however, the illustrations I have given, while serving their purpose, also furnished a fair idea of the development of style and variation of treatment of both the MS. and printed book under different influences, from the sixth to the close of the sixteenth century, but now I shall have to put on a pair of seven-league boots, and make some tremendous skips.

We have seen how, at the period of the early Renaissance, two streams met, as it were, and mingled, with very beautiful results. The freedom, the romance, the naturalism of the later Gothic, with the newly awakened Classical feeling, with its grace of line and mythological lore. The rich and delicate arabesques in which Italian designers delighted, and which so frequently decorated, as we have seen, the borders of the early printer, owe also something to Oriental influence, as indeed their name indicates. The decorative beauty of these early Renaissance books were really, therefore, the outcome of a very remarkable fusion of ideas and styles. Printing, as an art, and book decoration attained a perfection it has not since reached. The genius of the greatest designers of the time was associated with the new invention, and expressed itself with unparalleled vigour in the woodcut; while the type-founder, being still under the influence of a fine traditional style in handwriting, was in perfect harmony with the book decorator or illustrator. Even geometric diagrams were given without destroying the unity of the page, as may be seen in early editions of Euclid, and we have seen what faithful and characteristic work was done in illustrations of plants and animals, without loss of designing power and ornamental sense.

This happy equilibrium of artistic quality and practical adaptation after the middle of the sixteenth century began to decline. There were designers, like Oronce Finé and Geoffroy Tory, at Paris, who did much to preserve the traditions in book ornament of the early Italian printers, while adding a touch of grace and fancy of their own, but for the most part the taste of book designers ran to seed after this period. The classical influence, which had been only felt as one among other influences, became more and more paramount over the designer, triumphing over the naturalistic feeling, and over the Gothic and Eastern ornamental feeling; so that it might be said that, whereas Mediæval designers sought after colour and decorative beauty, Renaissance designers were influenced by considerations of line, form, and relief. This may have been due in a great measure to the fact that the influence of the antique and Classical art was a sculpturesque influence,

ORONTII
FINEI DELPHINATIS, RE-
GII MATHEMATICARVM
PROFESSORIS:

QVADRANS
ASTROLABICVS, OMNI-
bus Europæ regionibus inſeruiés:
Ex recenti & emédata ipſius Au-
thoris recognitione in ampliorē,
ac longè fideliorem redaċtus dc⸗
ſcriptionem.

PARISIIS.
Apud Simonem Colinæum.
1 5 3 4.

DESIGNED BY ORONCE FINÉ.   (PARIS, SIMON DE COLINES, 1534.)
(*Comp. Dürer's title to Plutarch, 1513, and St. Ambrosius, 1520.*)

mainly gathered from statues and relievos, gems
and medals, and architectural carved ornaments,
and more through Roman than Greek sources.
While suggestions from such sources were but
sparingly introduced at first, they gradually seemed
to outweigh all other motives with the later designers, whose works often suggest that it is
impossible to have too much Roman costume or
too many Roman remains, which crowd their Bible
subjects, and fill their borders with overfed pedi-
ments, corpulent scrolls, and volutes, and their
interstices with scattered fragments and attitudi-
nizing personifications of Classical mythology.
The lavish use of such materials were enough to
overweight even vigorous designers like Virgil
Solis, who though able, facile, and versatile as he
was, seems but a poor substitute for Holbein.

What was at first an inspiriting, imaginative,
and refining influence in art became finally a
destructive force. The youthful spirit of the early
Renaissance became clouded and oppressed, and
finally crushed with a weight of pompous pedantry
and affectation. The natural development of a
living style in art became arrested, and authority,
and an endeavour to imitate the antique, took its
place.

The introduction of the copper-plate marked a
new epoch in book illustration, and wood-engraving declined with its increased adoption, which, in
the form it took, as applied to books, in the seventeenth and eighteenth centuries, was certainly to
the detriment and final extinction of the decorative
side.

It has already been pointed out how a copper-plate, requiring a different process of printing, and exhibiting as a necessary consequence such different qualities of line and effect, cannot harmonize with type and the conditions of the surface-printed page, since it is not in any mechanical relation with them. This mechanical relation is really the key to all good and therefore organic design; and therefore it is that design was in sounder condition when mechanical conditions and relations were simpler. A new invention often has a dislocating effect upon design. A new element is introduced, valued for some particular facility or effect, and it is often adopted without considering how—like a new element in a chemical combination—it alters the relations all round.

Copper-plate engraving was presumably adopted as a method for book-illustration for its greater fineness and precision of line, and its greater command of complexity in detail and chiaroscuro, for its purely pictorial qualities, in short, and its adoption corresponded to the period of the ascendancy of the painter above other kind of artists.

As regards the books of the seventeenth century, while " of making many books there was no end," and however interesting for other than artistic reasons, but few would concern our immediate purpose. Wood-cuts, headings, initials, tail-pieces, and printers' ornaments continued to be used, but greatly inferior in design and beauty of effect to those of the sixteenth century. The copper-plates introduced are quite apart from the page ornaments, and can hardly be considered decorative, although in the pompous title-pages of books of this period they are frequently formal and archi-

VIRGIL SOLIS, BIBLE.

ARTIST UNKNOWN.   (VENICE, G. GIOLITO, 1562.)

tectural enough, and, as a rule, founded more or less upon the ancient arches of triumph of Imperial Rome.

Histories and philosophical works, especially towards the end of the seventeenth and beginning of the eighteenth centuries, were embellished with pompous portraits in frames of more or less classical joinery, with shields of arms, the worse for the decorative decline of heraldry, underneath. The specimen given is a good one of its type from a Venetian book of 1562, and gives the earlier form of this kind of treatment. Travels and topographical works increased, until by the middle of the eighteenth century we have them on the scale of Piranesi's scenic views of the architecture of ancient Rome.

The love of picturesqueness and natural scenery, or, perhaps, landscape gardening, gradually developing, concentrated interest on qualities the antithesis of constructive and inventive design, and drew the attention more and more away from them, until the painter, pure and simple, took all the artistic honours, and the days of the foundation of academies only confirmed and fixed the idea of art in this restricted sense in the public mind.

Hogarth, who availed himself of the copper-plate and publication in book form of his pictures, was yet wholly pictorial in his sympathies, and his instincts were dramatic and satiric rather than decorative. Able painter and designer as he was in his own way, the interest of his work is entirely on that side, and is rather valuable as illustrating the life and manners of his time than as furnishing examples of book illustration, and his work certainly has no decorative aim, although no doubt quite harmonious in an eighteenth century room.

Chodowiecki, who did a vast quantity of steel frontispieces and illustrations for books on a small scale, with plenty of character, must also be regarded rather as a maker of pictures for books than as a book decorator. He is sometimes mentioned as kindred in style to Stothard, but Stothard was much more of an idealist, and had, too, a very graceful decorative sense from the classical point of view. His book designs are very numerous, chiefly engraved on steel, and always showing a very graceful sense of line and composition. His designs to Rogers' " Poems," and " Italy," are well-known, and, in their earlier woodcut form, his groups of Amorini are very charming.

Flaxman had a high sense of sculpturesque style and simplicity, and great feeling and grace as a designer, but he can hardly be reckoned as a book decorator. His well-known series to Homer, Hesiod, Æschylus, and Dante are strictly distinct series of illustrative designs, to be taken by themselves without reference to their incorporation in, or relation to, a printed book. Their own lettering and explanatory text is engraved on the same plate beneath them, and so far they are consistent, but are not in any sense examples of page treatment or spacing.

We now come to a designer of a very different type, a type, too, of a new epoch, whatever resemblance in style and method there may be in his work to that of his contemporaries. William Blake is distinct, and stands alone. A poet and a seer,

A CRADLE SONG

Sweet dreams form a shade
O'er my lovely infants head
Sweet dreams of pleasant streams.
By happy silent moony beams

Sweet sleep with soft down.
Weave thy brows an infant crown.
Sweet sleep Angel mild
Hover o'er my happy child.

Sweet smiles in the night.
Hover over my delight.
Sweet smiles Mothers smiles
All the livelong night beguiles.

Sweet moans, dovelike sighs,
Chase not slumber from thy eyes,
Sweet moans, sweeter smiles.
All the dovelike moans beguiles.

Sleep sleep happy child.
All creation slept and smild.
Sleep sleep. happy sleep.
While o'er thee thy mother weep

Sweet babe in thy face.
Holy image I can trace.
Sweet babe once like thee.
Thy maker lay and wept for me

Wept

as well as a designer, in him seemed to awake something of the spirit of the old illuminator. He was not content to illustrate a book by isolated copper or steel plates apart from the text, although in his craft as engraver he constantly carried out the work of others. When he came to embody his own thoughts and dreams, he recurred quite spontaneously to the methods of the maker of the MS. books. He became his own caligrapher, illuminator and miniaturist, while availing himself of the copper-plate (which he turned into a surface printing block) and the printing press for the reproduction of his designs, and in some cases for producing them in tints. His hand-coloured drawings, the borderings and devices to his own poems, will always be things by themselves.

His treatment of the resources of black and white, and sense of page decoration, may be best judged perhaps by a reference to his " Book of Job," which contains a fine series of suggestive and imaginative designs. We seem to read in Blake something of the spirit of the Mediæval designers, through the sometimes mannered and semi-classic forms and treatment, according to the taste of his time ; while he embodies its more daring aspiring thoughts, and the desire for simpler and more humane conditions of life. A revolutionary fire and fervour constantly breaks out both in his verse and in his designs, which show very various moods and impulses, and comprehend a wide range of power and sympathy. Sometimes mystic and prophetic, sometimes tragic, sometimes simple and pastoral.

Blake, in these mixed elements, and the extraordinary suggestiveness of his work and the freedom of his thought, seems nearer to us than others of his contemporaries. In his sense of the decorative treatment of the page, too, his work bears upon our purpose. In writing with his own hand and in his own character the text of his poems, he gained the great advantage which has been spoken of—of harmony between text and illustration. They become a harmonious whole, in complete relation. His woodcuts to Phillip's " Pastoral," though per-

WILLIAM BLAKE.

WOODCUT FROM PHILLIP'S " PASTORAL."

haps rough in themselves, show what a sense of colour he could convey, and of the effective use of white line.

Among the later friends and disciples of Blake, a kindred spirit must have been Edward Calvert, whose book illustrations are also decorations ; the masses of black and white being effectively distributed, and they are full of poetic feeling, imagination, and sense of colour. I am indebted for the first knowledge of them to Mr. William Blake Richmond, whose father, Mr. George Richmond, was a friend of William Blake and Calvert, as well as of John Linnell and of Samuel Palmer, who carried on the traditions of this English poetic school to our own times; especially the latter, whose imaginative drawings — glowing sunsets over remote hill-tops, romantic landscapes, and pastoral sentiment—were marked features in the room of the Old Water Colour Society, up to his death in 1881. His etched illustrations to his edition of "The Eclogues of Virgil," are a fine series of beautifully designed and poetically conceived landscapes; but they are strictly a series of pictures printed separately from the text. Palmer himself, in the account of the work given by his son, when he was planning the work, wished that William Blake had been alive to have designed his woodcut headings to the "Eclogues."[1]

To Thomas Bewick and his school is due the revival of wood-engraving as an art, and its adaptation to book illustration, quite distinct, of course, from the old knife-work on the plank. Bewick had none of the imaginative poetry of the designers just named, although plenty of humour and satire, which he compressed into his little tailpieces. He shows his skill as a craftsman in the treatment of the wood block, in such works as his "British Birds;" but here, although the wood-engraving and type may be said to be in mechanical relation, there is no sense of decorative beauty or ornamental spacing whatever, and, as drawings, the engravings have none of the designer's power

[1] A memoir of Edward Calvert has since been published by his son, fully illustrated, and giving the little engravings just spoken of. They were engraved by Calvert himself, it appears, and I am indebted to his son, Mr. John Calvert, for permission to print them here.

THE
RETURN
HOME.

THE
FLOOD.

THE
CHAMBER
IDYLL.

FROM THE ORIGINAL BLOCKS DESIGNED AND ENGRAVED
ON WOOD BY EDWARD CALVERT.   BRIXTON, 1827-8-9.

THE
LADY
AND
THE
ROOKS.

IDEAL
PAST-
ORAL
LIFE.

THE
BROOK.

FROM THE BLOCKS DESIGNED AND ENGRAVED ON WOOD BY
EDWARD CALVERT.   BRIXTON, 1827-8-9

such as we found in the illustrations of Gesner and Matthiolus at Basle, in the middle of the sixteenth century. There is a very literal and plain presentment of facts as regards the bird and its plumage, but with scarcely more than the taste of the average stuffer and mounter in the composition of the picture, and no regard whatever to the design of the page as a whole.

It was, however, a great point to have asserted the claims of wood-engraving, and demonstrated its capabilities as a method of book illustration.

Bewick founded a school of very excellent craftsmen, who carried the art to a wonderful degree of finish. In both his and their hands it became quite distinct from literal translation of the drawing, which, unless in line, was treated by the engraver with a line, touch, and quality all his own, the use of white line,[1] and the rendering of tone and tint necessitating a certain power of design on his part, and giving him as important a position as the engraver on steel held in regard to the translation of a painted picture.

Such a book as Northcote's " Fables," published 1828-29, each fable having a head-piece drawn on wood from Northcote's design by William Harvey —a well-known graceful designer and copious illustrator of books up to comparatively recent times—and with initial letters and tail-pieces of his own, shows the outcome of the Bewick school. Finally " fineness of line, tone, and finish—a mis-

---

[1] A striking instance of the use of white line is seen in the title page " Pomerium de Tempore," printed by Johann Otmar, Augsburg, as early as 1502. It is possible, however, that this is a metal engraving. It is given overleaf.

used word," as Mr. W. J. Linton says, "was preferred to the simple charm of truth." The wood engravers appeared to be anxious to vie with the steel engravers in the adornment of books, and so far as adaptation was concerned, they had certainly all the advantage on their side. The ornamental sense, however, had everywhere declined; pictorial qualities, fineness of line, and delicacy of tone, were sought after almost exclusively.

Such books as Rogers's "Poems" and "Italy," with vignettes on steel from Thomas Stothard and J. M. W. Turner, are characteristic of the taste of the period, and show about the high-water mark of the skill of the book engravers on steel. Stothard's designs are the only ones which have claims to be decorative, and he is always a graceful designer. Turner's landscapes, exquisite in themselves, and engraved with marvellous delicacy, do not in any sense decorate the page, and from that point of view are merely shapeless blots of printers' ink of different tones upon it, while the letterpress bears no relation whatever to the picture in method of printing or design, and has no independent beauty of its own. Book illustrations of this type—and it was a type which largely prevailed during the second quarter of the century —are simply pictures without frames.

No survey of book illustration would be complete which contained no mention of William James Linton—whom I have already quoted. I may be allowed to speak of him with a peculiar regard and respect, as I may claim him as a very kind early friend and master. As a boy I was, in

Pomeriûm de tempore.
fratris Pelbarti ordinis sancti Francisci

JOHANN OTMAR.   (AUGSBURG, 1502.)

147

fact, apprenticed to him for the space of three years, not indeed with the object of wielding the graver, but rather with that of learning the craft of a draughtsman on wood. This, of course, was before the days of the use of photography, which has since practically revolutionized the system not only of drawing for books but of engraving also. It was then necessary to draw on the block itself, and to thoroughly understand what kind of work could be treated by the engraver.

I shall always regard those early years in Mr. Linton's office as of great value to me, as, despite changes of method and new inventions, it gave me a thorough knowledge of the mechanical conditions of wood-engraving at any rate, and has implanted a sense of necessary relationship between design, material, and method of production—of art and craft, in fact—which cannot be lost, and has had its effect in many ways.

Mr. Linton, too, is himself a notable historic link, carrying on the lamp of the older traditions of wood-engraving to these degenerate days, when whatever wonders of literal translation, and imitation of chalk, charcoal, or palette and brushes, it has exhibited under spell of American enterprise—and I am far from denying its achievements as such—it cannot be said to have preserved the distinction and independence of the engraver as an artist or original designer in any sense. When not extinguished altogether by some form of automatic reproductive process, he is reduced to the office of "process-server"—he becomes the slave of the pictorial artist. The picturesque sketcher loves his "bits" and "effects," which, moreover, however sensational and sparkling they may be in themselves, have no reference as a rule to the decoration of the page, being in this sense no more than more or less adroit splashes of ink upon it, which the text, torn into an irregularly ragged edge, seems instinctively to shrink from touching, squeezing itself together like the passengers in a crowded omnibus might do, reluctantly to admit a chimney-sweep.

While, by his early training and practice, he is united with the Bewick school, Mr. Linton—himself a poet, a social and political thinker, a scholar, as well as designer and engraver—having been associated with the best-known engravers and designers for books during the middle of the century, and having had art of such a different temper and tendency as that of Rossetti pass through his hands, and seen the effect of many new impulses, is finally face to face with what he himself has called the "American New Departure." He is therefore peculiarly and eminently qualified for the work to which he has addressed himself—his great work on "The Masters of Wood Engraving," which appeared in 1889, and is in every way complete as a history, learned in technique, and sumptuous as a book.

I have not mentioned Gustave Doré, who fills so large a space as an illustrator of books, because though possessed of a weird imagination, and a poetic feeling for dramatic landscapes and grotesque characters, as well as extraordinary pictorial invention, the mass of his work is purely scenic, and he never shows the decorative sense, or considers the design in relation to the page. His

149

best and most spirited and sincere work is represented by his designs in the " Contes Drolatiques."

The new movement in painting in England, known as the pre-Raphaelite movement, which dates from about the middle years of our century, was in every way so remarkable and far-reaching, that it is not surprising that it should leave its mark upon the illustrations of books; particularly upon that form of luxury known as the modern gift-book, which, in the course of the twenty years following 1850, often took the shape of selections from or editions of the poets plentifully sprinkled with little pictorial vignettes engraved on wood. Birket Foster, John Gilbert, and John Tenniel were leading contributors to these collections.

In 1857 appeared an edition of " Tennyson's Poems" from the house of Moxon. This work, while having the general characteristics of the prevailing taste—an accidental collection of designs, the work of designers of varying degrees of substance, temper, and feeling, casually arranged, and without the slightest feeling for page decoration or harmony of text and illustration—yet possessed one remarkable feature which gives it a distinction among other colleetions, in that it contains certain designs of the chief leaders of the pre-Raphaelite movement, D. G. Rossetti, Millais and Holman Hunt.

I give one of the Rossetti designs, " Sir Galahad"; the " S. Cecilia " and the " Morte d'Arthur " were engraved by the Brothers Dalziel, the " Sir Galahad " by Mr. W. J. Linton. It seems to me that the last gives the spirit and feeling of Rossetti, as well as his peculiar touch, far more

successfully. These designs, in their poetic imagination, their richness of detail, sense of colour, passionate, mystic, and romantic feeling, and earnestness of expression mark a new epoch. They are decorative in themselves, and, though quite distinct in feeling, and original, they are more akin to the work of the Mediæval miniaturist than anything that had been seen since his days. Even here, however, there is no attempt to consider the page or to make the type harmonize with the picture, or to connect it by any bordering or device with the book as a whole, and being sandwiched with drawings of a very different tendency, their effect is much spoiled. In one or two other instances where Rossetti lent his hand to book illustration, however, he is fully mindful of the decorative effect of the page. I remember a title page to a book of poems by Miss Christina Rossetti, "Goblin Market," which emphatically showed this. The title-page designed for his " Early Italian Poets " (given here), and his sonnet on the sonnet too, in which the design encloses the text of the poem, written out by himself, are other instances.

Some of the designs made for a later work (Dalziel's Bible Gallery, about 1865-70) also show the effect of the pre-Raphaelite influence, as well as, in the case of the designs of Sir Frederic Leighton and Mr. Poynter, the influence of Continental ideas and training. I saw some of these drawings on the wood at the time, I remember. For study and research, and richness of resource in archæological detail, as well as firmness of drawing, I thought Mr. Poynter's designs were perhaps the most remarkable. A strikingly realized picture,

THE EARLY ITALIAN POETS
from Ciullo d'Alcamo to Dante Alighieri
translated by D. Gabriel Rossetti.

London. Smith, Elder & Co. 1861

DESIGN FOR A TITLE PAGE.

and a bright and successful wood-engraving, is Ford Madox Brown's design of "Elijah and the Widow's Son." There is a dramatic intensity of expression about his other one also, " The Death of Eglon." Still, at best, we find that these are but carefully studied pictures rendered on the wood. The pre-Raphaelite designs show the most decorative sense, but they are now issued quite distinct from the page, whatever was the original intention, and while they may, as to scale and treatment, be justly considered as book illustrations, and as examples of our more important efforts in that direction at that time, they are not page decorations.

One may speak here of an admirable artist we have lost, Mr. Albert Moore, who so distinguished himself for his refined decorative sense in painting, and the outline group of figures given here shows that he felt the conditions of the book page and the press also.

Mr. Henry Holiday is also a decorative artist of great refinement and facility. He has not done very much in book illustration, but his illustrations to Lewis Carroll's " Hunting of the Snark" were admirable. His decorative feeling in black and white, however, is marked, as may be seen in the title to "Aglaia."

As, until recently, I suppose I was scarcely known out of the nursery, it is meet that I should offer some remarks upon children's books. Here, undoubtedly, there has been a remarkable development and great activity of late years. We all remember the little cuts that adorned the books of our childhood. The ineffaceable quality of these early pictorial and literary impressions afford

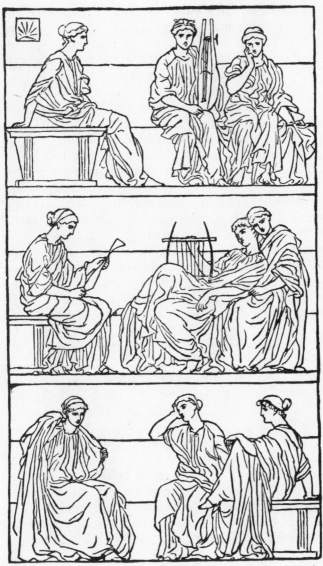

FROM MILTON'S ODE ON CHRIST'S NATIVITY.   (NISBET, 1867.)

the strongest plea for good art in the nursery and
the schoolroom. Every child, one might say
every human being, takes in more through his
eyes than his ears, and I think much more advantage might be taken of this fact.

If I may be personal, let me say that my first
efforts in children's books were made in association
with Mr. Edmund Evans. Here, again, I was
fortunate to be in association with the craft of
colour-printing, and I got to understand its possibilities. The books for babies, current at that
time—about 1865 to 1870—of the cheaper sort
called toy books were not very inspiriting. These
were generally careless and unimaginative woodcuts, very casually coloured by hand, dabs of pink
and emerald green being laid on across faces and
frocks with a somewhat reckless aim. There was
practically no choice between such as these and
cheap German highly-coloured lithographs. The
only attempt at decoration I remember was a set
of coloured designs to nursery rhymes by Mr. H.
S. Marks, which had been originally intended for
cabinet panels. Bold outlines and flat tints were
used. Mr. Marks has often shown his decorative
sense in book illustration and printed designs in
colour, but I have not been able to obtain any for
this book.

It was, however, the influence of some Japanese
printed pictures given to me by a lieutenant in the
navy, who had brought them home from there as
curiosities, which I believe, though I drew inspiration from many sources, gave the real impulse
to that treatment in strong outlines, and flat tints
and solid blacks, which I adopted with variations

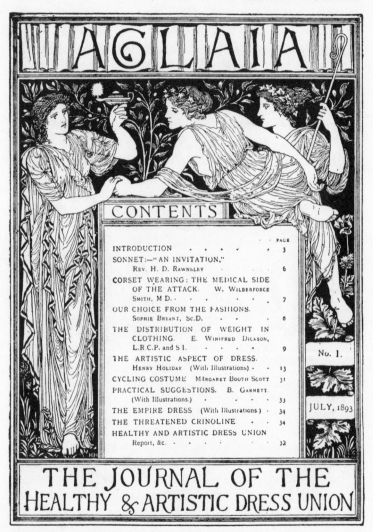

AGLAIA

CONTENTS

	PAGE
INTRODUCTION	3
SONNET:—"AN INVITATION." Rev. H. D. Rawnsley.	6
CORSET WEARING: THE MEDICAL SIDE OF THE ATTACK. W. Wilberforce Smith, M.D.	7
OUR CHOICE FROM THE FASHIONS. Sophie Bryant, Sc.D.	8
THE DISTRIBUTION OF WEIGHT IN CLOTHING. E. Winifred Dickson, L.R.C.P. and S I.	9
THE ARTISTIC ASPECT OF DRESS. Henry Holiday (With Illustrations)	13
CYCLING COSTUME Margaret Booth Scott	31
PRACTICAL SUGGESTIONS. B. Garnett. (With Illustrations.)	33
THE EMPIRE DRESS (With Illustrations)	34
THE THREATENED CRINOLINE	34
HEALTHY AND ARTISTIC DRESS UNION Report, &c.	32

No. 1.

JULY, 1893

THE JOURNAL OF THE
HEALTHY & ARTISTIC DRESS UNION

COVER FOR A MAGAZINE.

in books of this kind from that time (about 1870) onwards. Since then I have had many rivals for the favour of the nursery constituency, notably my late friend Randolph Caldecott, and Miss Kate Greenaway, though in both cases their aim lies more in the direction of character study, and their work is more of a pictorial character than strictly decorative. The little preface heading from his " Bracebridge Hall " gives a good idea of RANDOLPH CALDECOTT.

HEAD-PIECE TO "BRACEBRIDGE HALL."   (MACMILLAN, 1877.)

Caldecott's style when his aim was chiefly decorative. Miss Greenaway is the most distinctly so perhaps in the treatment of some of her calendars.

Children's books and so-called children's books hold a peculiar position. They are attractive to designers of an imaginative tendency, for in a sober and matter-of-fact age they afford perhaps the only outlet for unrestricted flights of fancy open to the modern illustrator, who likes to revolt against " the despotism of facts." While on children's books, the poetic feeling in the designs of E. V. B. may

be mentioned, and I mind me of some charming
illustrations to a book of Mr. George Macdonald's,
KATE GREENAWAY.

KEY BLOCK OF TITLE-PAGE OF "MOTHER GOOSE."
(ROUTLEDGE, N.D.)

" At the Back of the North Wind," designed by
Mr. Arthur Hughes, who in these and other wood

engraved designs shows, no less than in his paintings, how refined and sympathetic an artist he is. Mr. Robert Bateman, too, designed some charming little woodcuts, full of poetic feeling and controlled by unusual taste. They were used in Macmillan's "Art at Home" series, though not, I believe, originally intended for it.

ARTHUR HUGHES.

FROM "AT THE BACK OF THE NORTH WIND." (STRAHAN, 1871.)

There is no doubt that the opening of Japanese ports to Western commerce, whatever its after effects — including its effect upon the arts of Japan itself — has had an enormous influence on European and American art. Japan is, or was, a country very much, as regards its arts and handicrafts with the exception of architecture, in the condition of a European country in the Middle Ages, with wonderfully skilled artists and craftsmen in all manner of work of the decorative kind, who were under the influence of a free and informal naturalism. Here at least was a living art, an art of the people, in which traditions and craftsmanship were unbroken, and the results full of attractive variety, quickness, and naturalistic force. What wonder that it took Western artists by storm, and that its effects have become so patent, though not always happy, ever since. We see unmistakable traces of Japanese influences, however, almost everywhere — from the Parisian impressionist painter to the Japanese fan in the corner of trade circulars, which shows it has been adopted as a stock printers' ornament. We see it in

ARTHUR HUGHES.

FROM "AT THE BACK OF THE NORTH WIND." (STRAHAN, 1871.)

the sketchy blots and lines, and vignetted naturalistic flowers which are sometimes offered as page decorations, notably in American magazines and fashionable etchings. We have caught the vices of Japanese art certainly, even if we have assimilated some of the virtues.

In the absence of any really noble architecture

or substantial constructive sense, the Japanese artists are not safe guides as designers. They may be able to throw a spray of leaves or a bird or fish across a blank panel or sheet of paper, drawing them with such consummate skill and certainty that it may delude us into the belief that it is decorative design; but if an artist of less skill essays to do the like the mistake becomes obvious. Granted they have a decorative sense — the *finesse* which goes to the placing of a flower in a pot, of hanging a garland on a wall, or of placing a mat or a fan — taste, in short, that is a different thing from real constructive power of design, and satisfactory filling of spaces.

ROBERT BATEMAN.

FROM "ART IN THE HOUSE."
(MACMILLAN, 1876.)

When we come to their books, therefore, marvellous as they are, and full of beauty and suggestion—apart from their naturalism, *grotesquerie*, and humour—they do not furnish fine examples of page decoration as a rule. The fact that their text is written vertically, however, must be allowed for. This, indeed, converts their page into a panel, and their printed books become rather what we should consider sets of designs for decorating light panels, and extremely charming as such.

These drawings of Hokusai's (see Nos. 10 and 11, Appendix), the most vigorous and prolific of the more modern and popular school, are striking enough and fine enough, in their own way, and the decorative sense is never absent; controlled, too, by the dark border-line, they do fill the page, which is not the case always with the flowers and birds. However, I believe these holes, blanks, and spaces to let are only tolerable in a book because the drawing where it does occur is so skilful (except where the effect is intentionally open and light); and from tolerating we grow to like them, I suppose, and take them for signs of

ROBERT BATEMAN.

FROM "ART IN THE HOUSE."
(MACMILLAN, 1877.)

mastery and decorative skill. In their smaller applied ornamental designs, however, the Japanese often show themselves fully aware of a systematic plan or geometric base : and there is usually some hidden geometric relation of line in some of their apparently accidental compositions. Their books of crests and pattern plans show indeed a careful study of geometric shapes, and their controlling influence in designing.

As regards the history and use of printing, the Japanese had it from the Chinese, who invented the art of printing from wooden blocks in the sixth century. "We have no record," says Professor Douglas,[1] "as to the date when metal type was first used in China, but we find Korean books printed as early as 1317 with movable clay or wooden type, and just a century later we have a record of a fount of metal type being cast to print

ROBERT BATEMAN.

FROM "ART IN THE HOUSE."
(MACMILLAN, 1876.)

an "Epitome of the Eighteen Historical Records of China." Printing is supposed to have been adopted in Japan "after the first invasion of the Korea by the armies of Hideyoshi, in the end of the sixteenth century, when large quantities of movable type books were brought back by one of his generals, which formed the model upon which the Japanese worked."[2]

I have mentioned the American development of wood-engraving. Its application to magazine illustration seems certainly to have developed or to have occured with the appearance of very clever draughtsmen from the picturesque and literal point of view.

[1] Guide to the Chinese and Japanese Illustrated Books in the British Museum.
[2] Satow. "History of Printing in Japan."

The admirable and delicate architectural and landscape drawings of Mr. Joseph Pennell, for instance, are well known, and, as purely illustrative work, fresh, crisp in drawing, and original in treatment, giving essential points of topography and local characteristics (with a happy if often quaint and unexpected selection of point of view, and pictorial limits), it would be difficult to find their match, but very small consideration or consciousness is shown for the page. If he will pardon my saying so, in some instances the illustrations are, or used to be, often daringly driven through the text, scattering it right and left, like the effect of a coach and four upon a flock of sheep. In some of his more recent work, notably in his bolder drawings such as those in the " Daily Chronicle," he appears to have considered the type relation much more, and shows, especially in some of his skies, a feeling for a radiating arrangement of line.

ROBERT BATEMAN.

FROM "ART IN THE HOUSE."
(MACMILLAN, 1876.)

Our American cousins have taught us another mode of treatment in magazine pages. It is what I have elsewhere described as the "card-basket style." A number of naturalistic sketches are thrown accidentally together, the upper ones hiding the under ones partly, and to give variety the corner is occasionally turned down. There has been a great run on this idea of late years, but I fancy it is a card trick about "played out."

However opinions may vary, I think there cannot be a doubt that in Elihu Vedder we have an instance of an American artist of great imaginative powers, and undoubtedly a designer of originality and force. This is sufficiently proved from his large work—the illustrations to the "Rubaiyat of Omar Khayyam." Although the designs have no Persian character about them which one would have thought the poem and its imagery would naturally have suggested, yet they are a fine series, and show much decorative sense and dramatic power, and are quite modern in feeling. His designs for the cover of "The Century Magazine" show taste and decorative feeling in the combination of figures with lettering.

Mr. Edwin Abbey is another able artist, who has shown considerable care for his illustrated page, in some cases supplying his own lettering; though he has been growing more pictorial of late: Mr. Alfred Parsons also, though he too often seems more drawn to the picture than the decoration. Mr. Heywood Sumner shows a charming decorative sense and imaginative feeling, as well as humour. On the purely ornamental side, the accomplished decorations of Mr. Lewis Day exhibit both ornamental range and resource, which, though in general devoted to other objects, are conspicuous enough in certain admirable book and magazine covers he has designed.

FROM "STORIES FOR CHILDREN," BY FRANCES M. PEARD. (ALLEN, 1896.)

ILLUSTRATION TO "THE GOOD FIGHT." ("ONCE A WEEK," 1859.)

(By permission of Messrs. Bradbury, Agnew and Co.)

169

THE "ENGLISH ILLUSTRATED MAGAZINE."

"The English Illustrated Magazine," under Mr. Comyns Carr's editorship, by its use of both old and modern headings, initials and ornaments, did something towards encouraging the taste for decorative design in books. Among the artists who designed pages therein should be named

HEYWOOD SUMNER.

FROM "STORIES FOR CHILDREN," BY F. M. PEARD.   (ALLEN, 1896.

Henry Ryland and Louis Davis, both showing graceful ornamental feeling, the children of the latter artist being very charming.

But it would need much more space to attempt to do justice to the ability of my contemporaries, especially in the purely illustrative division, than I am able to give.

The able artists of "Punch," however, from John Leech to Linley Sambourne, have done much to keep alive a vigorous style of drawing in line, which, in the case of Mr. Sambourne, is united

Sleep, baby, sleep! the Mother sings:
Heaven's angels kneel and fold their wings.
Sleep, baby, sleep!

With swathes of scented hay thy bed
By Mary's hand at eve was spread.
Sleep, baby, sleep!

At midnight came the shepherds, they
Whom seraphs wakened by the way.
Sleep, baby, sleep!

And three kings from the East afar
Ere dawn came guided by a star.
Sleep, baby, sleep!

They brought thee gifts of gold and gems
Rich orient pearls, pure diadems.
Sleep, baby, sleep!

But thou who liest slumbering there
Art King of kings, earth, ocean, air.
Sleep, baby, sleep!

Sleep, baby, sleep! the shepherds sing:
Through heaven, through earth, hosannas ring.
Sleep, baby, sleep!

John. Addington. Symonds.

FROM THE "ENGLISH ILLUSTRATED MAGAZINE" (1892).

with great invention, graphic force, and designing power. In speaking of "Punch," one ought not to forget either the important part played by "Once a Week" in introducing many first-rate artists in line. In its early days we had Charles Keene illustrating Charles Reade's "Good Fight," with much feeling for the decorative effect of the old German woodcut. Such admirable artists as M. J. Lawless and Frederick Sandys—the latter especially distinguished for his splendid line drawings in "Once a Week" and "The Cornhill;" one of his finest is here given, "The Old Chartist," which accompanied a poem by Mr. George Meredith. Indeed, it is impossible to speak too highly of Mr. Sandys' draughtsmanship and power of expression by means of line; he is one of our modern English masters who has never, I think, had justice done to him.

I can only just briefly allude to certain powerful and original modern designers of Germany, where indeed, the old vigorous traditions of woodcut and illustrative drawing seem to have been kept more unbroken than elsewhere.

On the purely character-drawing, pictorial and illustrative side, there is of course Menzel, thoroughly modern, realistic, and dramatic. I am thinking more perhaps of such men as Alfred Rethel, whose designs of "Death the Friend" and "Death the Enemy," two large woodcuts, are well known. I remember also a very striking series of designs of his, a kind of modern "Dance of Death," which appeared about 1848, I think. Schwind is another whose designs to folk tales are thoroughly German in spirit and imagination, and style of drawing.

Forget not yet the tried intent
Of such a truth as I have meant
My great travail so gladly spent
Forget not yet

Forget not yet when first began
The weary life ye know since when
The suit the service none tell can
Forget not yet

Forget not yet the great assays
The cruel wrong the scornful ways
The painful patience in delays
Forget not yet

Forget not! O forget not this
How long ago hath been and is
The mind that never meant amiss
Forget not yet

Forget not then thine own approved
The which so long hath thee so loved
Whose steadfast faith yet never moved
Forget not yet
Sir Thomas Wyat.

FROM THE "ENGLISH ILLUSTRATED MAGAZINE" (1894).

Oscar Pletsch, too, is remarkable for his feeling for village life and children, and many of his illustrations have been reproduced in this country. More recent evidence, and more directly in the decorative direction, of the vigour and ornamental skill of German designers, is to be found in those picturesque calendars, designed by Otto Hupp, which come from Munich, and show something very like the old feeling of Burgmair, especially in the treatment of the heraldry.

I have ventured to give a page or two here from my own books, "Grimm," "The Sirens Three," and others, which serve at least to show two very different kinds of page treatment. In the "Grimm" the picture is inclosed in formal and rectangular lines, with medallions of flowers at the four corners, the title and text being written on scrolls above and below. In "The Sirens Three" a much freer and more purely ornamental treatment is adopted, and a bolder and more open line. A third, the frontispiece of "The Necklace of Princess Fiorimonde," by Miss de Morgan, is more of a simple pictorial treatment, though strictly decorative in its scheme of line and mass.

The facile methods of photographic-automatic reproduction certainly give an opportunity to the designer to write out his own text in the character that pleases him, and that accords with his design, and so make his page a consistent whole from a decorative point of view, and I venture to think when this is done a unity of effect is gained for the page not possible in any other way.

Indeed, the photograph, with all its allied

("ONCE A WEEK," 1861.)

"THE OLD CHARTIST."

"DEAD LOVE."

discoveries and its application to the service of the printing press, may be said to be as important a discovery in its effects on art and books as was the discovery of printing itself. It has already largely transformed the system of the production of illustrations and designs for books, magazines, and newspapers, and has certainly been the means of securing to the artist the advantage of possession of his original, while its fidelity, in the best processes, is, of course, very valuable.

Its influence, however, on artistic style and treatment has been, to my mind, of more doubtful advantage. The effect on painting is palpable enough, but so far as painting becomes photographic, the advantage is on the side of the photograph. It has led in illustrative work to the method of painting in black and white, which has taken the place very much of the use of line, and through this, and by reason of its having fostered and encouraged a different way of regarding nature —from the point of view of accidental aspect, light and shade, and tone—it has confused and deteriorated, I think, the faculty of inventive design, and the sense of ornament and line; having concentrated artistic interest on the literal realization of certain aspects of superficial facts, and instantaneous impressions instead of ideas, and the abstract treatment of form and line.

This, however, may be as much the tendency of an age as the result of photographic invention, although the influence of the photograph must count as one of the most powerful factors of that tendency. Thought and vision divide the world of art between them—our thoughts follow our

WALTER CRANE.

· THE ·
· SLEEPING ·
· BEAUTY ·

" -· AT· LAST· HE· CAME· TO· THE·
·TOWER· & OPENED· THE· DOOR·
· OF· THE· LITTLE· ROOM· WHERE·
· ROSAMOND· LAY· "

FROM GRIMM'S "HOUSEHOLD STORIES."   (MACMILLAN, 1882.)

THE · SIRENS · THREE

OST on a sleepless sea, without avail
My soul's ship drifted wide, with idle sail
And slow pulsating oars, that night's blue gulf
Beat noiselessly to Time's recurring tale.

II
The rolling hours like waves broke, one by one,
Upon the tide of thought time's sands outrun,
And cloudy visions hovered o'er my bed,
Piled to the stars, full soon like cloud undone:

III
As, like the wan moon through her fleecy sea,
My spirit clove their rack unceasingly,
And struck at last upon an unknown ground,
More still than sleep, more strange than dreamlands be.

"THE SIRENS THREE" OPENING PAGE. (MACMILLAN, 1886.)

vision, our vision is influenced by our thoughts. A book may be the home of both thought and vision. Speaking figuratively, in regard to book decoration, some are content with a rough shanty in the woods, and care only to get as close to nature in her more superficial aspects as they can. Others would surround their house with a garden indeed, but they demand something like an architectural plan. They would look at a frontispiece like a façade; they would take hospitable encouragement from the title-page as from a friendly inscription over the porch; they would hang a votive wreath at the dedication, and so pass on into the hall of welcome, take the author by the hand and be led by him and his artist from room to room, as page after page is turned, fairly decked and adorned with picture, and ornament, and device; and, perhaps, finding it a dwelling after his desire, the guest is content to rest in the ingle nook in the firelight of the spirit of the author or the play of fancy of the artist; and, weaving dreams in the changing lights and shadows, to forget life's rough way and the tempestuous world outside.

CHAPTER IV. OF THE RECENT DE-VELOPMENT OF DECORATIVE BOOK ILLUSTRATION AND THE MODERN REVIVAL OF PRINTING AS AN ART.

INCE the three Cantor Lectures, which form the substance of the foregoing chapters, were delivered by me at the rooms of the Society of Arts, some six or seven years have elapsed, and they have been remarkable for a pronounced revival of activity and interest in the art of the printer and the decorative illustrator, the paper-maker, the binder, and all the crafts connected with the production of tasteful and ornate books.

Publishers and printers have shown a desire to return to simpler and earlier standards of taste, and in the choice and arrangement of the type to take a leaf out of the book of some of the early professors of the craft. There has been a passion for tall copies and handmade paper; for delicate bindings, and first editions.

There has grown up, too, quite a literature about the making of the book beautiful—whereof the Ex-Libris Series alone is witness. We have, besides, the history of Early Printed Books by Mr. Gordon Duff, of Early Illustrated Books by Mr. Pollard. The Book-plate has been looked after by Mr. Egerton Castle, and by a host of eager collectors ever since. Mr. Pennell is well known as the tutelary genius who takes charge of illustrators, and discourses upon them at large, and Mr. Strange bids us, none too soon, to become acquainted with our alphabets. I have not yet heard of any specialist taking up his parable upon "end papers," but, altogether, the book has never perhaps had so much writing outside of it, as it were, before.

A brilliant band of illustrators and ornamentists have appeared, too, and nearly every month or so we hear of a new genius in black and white, who is to eclipse all others. For all that, even in the dark ages, between the mid-nineteenth century and the early eighties, one or two printers or publishers of taste have from time to time attempted to restrain the wild excesses of the trade-printer, with his terribly monotonous novelties in founts of type, alternately shouting or whispering, anon in the crushing and aggressive heaviness of block capitals, and now in the attenuated droop of italics. Sad havoc has been played with the decorative dignity of the page, indeed, as well as with the form and breed of roman and gothic letters : one might have imagined that some mischievous printer's devil had thrown the apple of discord among the letters of the alphabet, so ingeniously ugly were so many modern so-called "fancy" types.

We have had good work from the Edinburgh houses, from Messrs. R. and R. Clark, and Messrs. Constable, and in London from the Chiswick Press, for instance, ever since the old days of its connection with the tasteful and well printed volumes from the house of Pickering. Various artists, too, in association with their book designs, from D. G. Rossetti onwards, have designed their own lettering to be in decorative harmony with their designs. The Century Guild, with its " Hobby Horse" and its artists, like Mr. Horne

FROM TITLE-PAGE. "THE SCOTTISH ART REVIEW" (SCOTT, 1889).

and Mr. Selwyn Image, did much to keep alive true taste in printing and book decoration, when they were but little understood.[1] There have been printers, too, such as Mr. Daniel at Oxford, and De Vinne at New York, who have from different points of view brought care and selection to the choice of type and the printing of books, and have adapted or designed type.

But the field for extensive artistic experiment in these directions was tolerably clear when Mr. William Morris turned his attention to printing, and, in 1891, founded the Kelmscott Press.

So far as I am aware, he has been the first to approach the craft of practical printing from the point of view of the artist, and although, no doubt, the fact of being a man of letters as well was an extra advantage, his particular success in the art of printing is due to the former qualification. A long and distinguished practice as a designer in other matters of decorative art brought him to the nice questions of type design, its place upon the page, and its relation to printed ornament and illustration, peculiarly well equipped; while his historic knowledge and discrimination, and the possession of an extraordinarily rich and choice collection of both mediæval MSS. and early printed books afforded him an abundant choice of the best models.

In the results which have been produced at the

[1] And they elicited a response from across the water in the shape of "The Knight Errant," the work of a band of young enthusiasts at Boston, Mass., of which Mr. Lee and Mr. Goodhue may be named as leading spirits—the latter being the designer of the cover of "The Knight Errant," and the former the printer.

Kelmscott press we trace the effect of all these
influences, acting under the strongest personal
predilection, and a mediæval bias (in an artistic
sense) which may be said to be almost exclusive.

The Kelmscott roman type ("golden") perhaps
rather suggests that it was designed to anticipate
and to provide against the demand of readers or
book fanciers who could stand nothing else than
roman, while the heart of the printer really
hankered after black letter. But compare this
"golden" type with most modern lower case
founts, up to the date of its use, and its advan-
tages both in form and substance are remarkable.
Modern type, obeying, I suppose, a resistless
law of evolution, had reached, especially with
American printers, the last stage of attenuation.
The type of the Kelmscott press is an emphatic
and practical protest against this attenuation ; just
as its bold black and white ornaments and decorative woodcuts in open line are protests against
the undue thinness, atmospheric effect, and dia-
phanous vignetting by photographic process and
tone-block of much modern illustration, which
may indeed *illustrate*, but does not *ornament* a
book. The paper, too, hand-made, rough-surfaced,
and tough, is in equally strong contrast to the
shiny hot-pressed machine-made paper, hitherto
so much in vogue for the finer kinds of printing,
and by which it alone became possible. The two
kinds—the two ideals of printing—are as far apart
as the poles. Those who like the smooth and
thin, will not like the bold and rough ; but it looks
as if the Kelmscott standard had marked the turn
of the tide, and that, judging from the signs of its

Chapter II. Evil tidings come to hand at Cleveland.

NOT long had he worked ere he heard the sound of horse-hoofs once more, and he looked not up, but said to himself, "It is but the lads bringing back the teams from the acres, and riding fast and driving hard for joy of heart and in wantonness of youth". But the sound grew nearer and he looked up and saw over the turf wall of the garth the

influence upon printers and publishers generally, the feeling is running strongly in that direction. (One would think the human eyesight would benefit also.) This is the more remarkable since the Kelmscott books are by no means issued at "popular prices," are limited in number, and for the most part are hardly for the general reader—unless that ubiquitous person is more erudite and omnivorous than is commonly credited.

Books, however, which may be called monumental in the national and general sense, have been printed at the Kelmscott press, such as Shakespeare's "Poems," More's "Utopia"; and Mr. Morris's *magnum opus*, the folio Chaucer, enriched by the designs of Burne-Jones, has recently been completed.[1]

In Mr. Morris's ornaments and initials, nearly always admirably harmonious in their quantities with the character and mass of the type, we may perhaps trace mixed influences in design. In the rich black and white scroll and floral borders surrounding the title and first pages, we seem to see the love of close-filling and interlacement characteristic of Celtic and Byzantine work, with a touch of the feeling of the practical textile designer, which comes out again in the up-and-down, detached bold page ornaments, though here combined with suggestions from early English illuminated MS.

These influences, however, only add to the

---

[1] Completed, indeed, it might almost be said, with the life of the craftsman. It is sad to have to record, while these pages were passing through the press, our master printer—one of the greatest Englishmen of our time—is no more.

distinctive character and richness of the effect, and no attempt is made to get beyond the simple conditions of bold black and white designs for the woodcut and the press.

Mr. Morris adopts the useful canon in printing that the true page is what the open book displays —what is generally termed a double page. He considers them practically as two columns of type, necessarily separate owing to the construction of the book, but together as it lies open, forming a page of type, only divided by the narrow margin where the leaves are inserted in the back of the covers. We thus get the *recto* and the *verso* pages or columns, each with their distinctive proportions of margin, as they turn to the right or the left from the centre of the book—the narrowest margins being naturally inwards and at the top, the broadest those outwards and at the foot, which latter should be deepest of all. It may be called *the handle* of the book, and there is reason in the broad margin, though also gracious to the eye, since the hand may hold the book without covering any of the type.

It is really the due consideration of the necessity of these little utilities in the construction and use of a thing which enables the modern designer— separated as he is from the actual maker—to preserve that distinctive and organic character in any work so valuable, and always so fruitful in artistic suggestion, and this I think holds true of all design in association with handicraft.

The more immediate and intimate—one might occasionally say imitative—influence of the Kelmscott press may be seen in the extremely

C. M. GERE.

MIDSUMMER

Crown of the year how fair thou shinest
How little in thy pride divinest
Inevitable fall.

LANDOR

FROM THE "ENGLISH ILLUSTRATED MAGAZINE" (1893).

FROM "HANS ANDERSEN." (ALLEN, 1893.)

BRIDGE St
EVESHAM:

E H N

PROCESS BLOCK FROM THE ORIGINAL PEN DRAWING.

interesting work of a group of young artists who own their training to the Birmingham School of Art, as developed under the taste and ability of Mr. Taylor. Three of these, Mr. C. M. Gere, Mr. E. H. New, and Mr. Gaskin, have designed illustrations for some of Mr. Morris's Kelmscott books, so that the connection of ideas is perfectly sequent and natural, and it is only as might be expected that the school should have the courage of their artistic opinions, and boldly carry into practice the results of their Kelmscott inspirations, by printing a journal themselves, "The Quest."

Mr. Gere, Mr. Gaskin, and Mr. New may be said to be the leaders of the Birmingham School. Mr. Gere has engraved on wood some of his own designs, and he thoroughly realizes the ornamental value of bold and open line drawing in association with lettering, and is a careful and conscientious draughtsman and painter besides. A typical instance of his work is the "Finding of St. George."

Mr. Gaskin's Christmas book, "King Wenceslas," is, perhaps, his best work so far as we have seen. The designs are simple and bold, and in harmony with the subject, and good in decorative character. His illustrations to Hans Christian Andersen's "Fairy Tales" are full of a naïve romantic feeling, and have much sense of the decorative possibilities of black and white drawing. Mrs. Gaskin's designs for children's books show a quaint fancy and ornamental feeling characteristic of the school.

Mr. New's feeling is for quaint streets and old buildings, which he draws with conscientious thoroughness, and attention to characteristic details of construction and local variety, without any reliance on accidental atmospheric effects, but using a firm open line and broad, simple arrangements of light and shade, which give them a decorative look as book illustrations.   It is owing

INIGO THOMAS.

GARDEN GATE : AVEBURY : WILTSHIRE

FROM "THE FORMAL GARDEN."   (MACMILLAN, 1892.)

to these qualities that they are ornamental, and not to any actual ornament.   Indeed, in those cases where he has introduced borders to frame his pictures, he does not seem to me to be so successful as an ornamentist pure and simple, though in his latest work, the illustrations to Mr. Lane's edition of Isaac Walton's "Compleat Angler," there are pretty headings and tasteful title scrolls, as well as good drawings of places.

The question of border is, however, always a most difficult one.   One might compare the illus-

204

SUNDIAL : WREST : BEDFORDSHIRE

FROM "THE FORMAL GARDEN." (MACMILLAN, 1892.)

trative drawings of architecture and gardens of Mr. Inigo Thomas in Mr. Reginald Blomfield's work on gardens, with Mr. New, as showing, with considerable decorative feeling, and feeling for the subject, a very different method of drawing, one might say more pictorial in a sense, the line being much thinner and closer, and in effect greyer and darker. The introduction of the titles helps the ornamental effect.

Among the leading artists of the Birmingham School must be mentioned Mr. H. Payne, Mr. Bernard Sleigh and Mr. Mason for their romantic feeling in story illustrations; Miss Bradley for her inventive treatment of crowds and groups of children; Miss Winifred Smith for her groups of children and quaint feeling; Mrs. Arthur Gaskin also for her pretty quaint fancies in child-life; Miss Mary Newill for her ornamental rendering of natural landscape, as in the charming drawing of Porlock; and Miss Celia Levetus for her decorative feeling. It may, at any rate, I think be claimed for it, that both in method, sentiment, and subject, it is peculiarly English, and represents a sincere attempt to apply what may be called traditional principles in decoration to book illustration.

Among the recent influences tending to foster the feeling for the treatment of black and white design and book illustrations, *primarily from the decorative point of view*, the Arts and Crafts Exhibition Society may claim to have had some share, and they have endeavoured, by the tendency of the work selected for exhibition as well as by papers and lectures by various members on this point, to emphasize its importance and to spread

clear principles, even at the risk of appearing
partial and biased in one direction, and leaving
many clever artists in black and white unrepre-
sented.

Now for graphic ability, originality, and variety,
there can be no doubt of the vigour of our modern
black and white artists. It is the most vital and
really popular form of art at the present day, and
it, far more than painting, deals with the actual
life of the people; it is, too, thoroughly demo-
cratic in its appeal, and, associated with the newspaper and magazine, goes everywhere—at least, as
far as there are shillings and pence—and where
often no other form of art is accessible.

But graphic power and original point of view is
not always associated with the decorous ornamental
sense. It is, in fact, often its very antithesis,
although, on the other hand, good graphic drawing, governed by a sense of style to which economy
or simplicity of line often leads, has ornamental
quality.

I should say at once that sincere graphic or
naturalistic drawing, with individual character and
style, is always preferable to merely lifeless, purely
imitative, and tame repetition in so-called decorative work.

While I claim that certain decorative considerations such as plan, scale balance, proportion,
quantity, relation to type, are essential to really
beautiful book illustration, I do not in the least
wish to ignore the clever work of many contemporary illustrators because they only care to be
illustrators pure and simple, and prefer to consider
a page of paper, or any part of it unoccupied by

FROM "A BOOK OF CAROLS."   (ALLEN, 1893.)

F. MASON.

FROM "HUON OF BORDEAUX." (ALLEN, 1895.)

GERTRUDE M. BRADLEY.

THE CHERRY FESTIVAL.

(FROM A PEN DRAWING.)

213

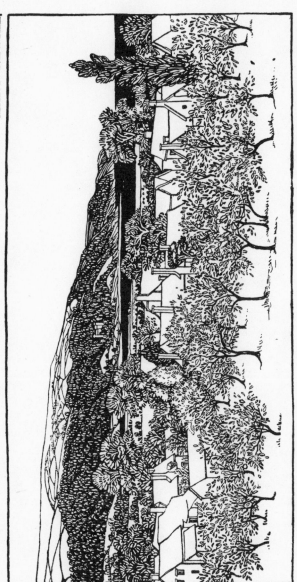

MARY NEWILL.

PORLOCK.

(FROM A PEN DRAWING.)

215

type, as a fair field for a graphic sketch, with no more consideration for its relation to the page itself or the rest of the book, than an artist usually feels when he jots down something from life in his sketch-book.

CELIA LEVETUS.

A BOOKPLATE.

I think that book illustration should be something more than a collection of accidental sketches. Since one cannot ignore the constructive organic element in the formation — the idea of the book itself — it is so far inartistic to leave it out of account in designing work intended to form an essential or integral part of that book.

I do not, however, venture to assert that decorative illustration can only be done in *one* way—if so, there would be an end in that direction to originality or individual feeling. There is nothing absolute in art, and one cannot dogmatize, but it seems to me that in all designs certain conditions must be acknowledged, and not only acknowledged but accepted freely, just as one would accept the rules of a game before attempting to play it.

The rules, the conditions of a sport or game, give it its own peculiar character and charm, and by means of them the greatest amount of pleasure and keenest excitement is obtained in the long run, just as by observing the conditions, the limitations of an art or handicraft, we shall extract the greatest amount of pleasure for the worker and beauty for the beholder.

Many remarkable designers in black and white of individuality and distinction, and with more or less strong feeling for decorative treatment, have arisen during the last few years. Among these ought to be named Messrs. Ricketts and Shannon, whose joint work upon "The Dial" is sufficiently well known. They, too, have taken up printing as an art, Mr. Ricketts having designed his own type and engraved his own drawings on wood. They are excellent craftsmen as well as inventive and original artists of remarkable cultivation, imaginative feeling and taste. There is a certain suggestion of inspiration from William Blake in Mr. Shannon sometimes, and of German or Italian fifteenth century woodcuts in the work of Mr. Ricketts. The weird designs of Mr. Reginald Savage should also be noted, as well as the charming woodcuts of Mr. Sturge Moore.

Another very remarkable designer in black and white is Mr. Aubrey Beardsley. His work shows a delicate sense of line, and a bold decorative use of

HERO AND LEANDER BY CHRISTOPHER MARLOWE AND GEORGE CHAPMAN

Hero's description and her love's;
The fane of Venus where he moves
His worthy love-suit, and attains;
Whose bliss the wrath of Fates restrains
For Cupid's grace to Mercury:
Which tale the author doth imply.

FROM "HERO AND LEANDER."   (THE VALE PRESS.)

solid blacks, as well as an extraordinarily weird fancy and grotesque imagination, which seems occasionally inclined to run in a morbid direction. Although, as in the case of most artists, one can trace certain influences which have helped in the formation of their style, there can be no doubt of his individuality and power. The designs for the work by which Mr. Beardsley became first known, I believe, the "Morte d'Arthur," alone are sufficient to show this. There appears to be a strong mediæval decorative feeling, mixed with a curious weird Japanese-like spirit of *diablerie* and grotesque, as of the opium-dream, about his work; but considered as book-decoration, though it is effective, the general abstract treatment of line, and the use of large masses of black and white, rather suggest designs intended to be carried out in some other material, such as inlay or enamel, for instance, in which they would gain the charm of beautiful surface and material, and doubtless look very well. Mr. Beardsley shows different influences in his later work in the "Savoy," some of which suggests a study of eighteenth century designers, such as Callot or Hogarth, and old English mezzotints.

"The Studio," which, while under the able and sympathetic editorship of Mr. Gleeson White, first called attention (by the medium of Mr. Pennell's pen) to Mr. Beardsley's work, has done good service in illustrating the progress of decorative art, both at home and abroad, and has from time to time introduced several young artists whose designs have thus become known to the public for the first time, such as Mr. Patten Wilson, Mr.

Laurence Housman, Mr. Fairfax Muckley, and Mr. Charles Robinson, who all have their own distinctive feeling : the first for bold line drawings after the old German method with an abundance of detail ; the second for remarkable taste in ornament, and a humorous and poetic fancy ; the third for a very graceful feeling for line and the decorative use of black and white—especially in the treatment of trees and branch work, leaves and flowers associated with figures.

Mr. J. D. Batten has distinguished himself for some years past as an inventive illustrator of Fairy Tales. In his designs, perhaps, he shows more of the feeling of the story-teller than the decorator in line, on the whole ; his feeling as a painter, perhaps, not making him quite content with simple black and white ; and, certainly, his charming tempera picture of the sleeping maid and the dwarfs, and his excellent printed picture of Eve and the serpent, printed by Mr. Fletcher in the Japanese method, might well excuse him if that is the case.

Mr. Henry Ford is another artist who has devoted himself with much success to Fairy Tale pictures in black and white, being associated with the fairy books of many different colours issued under the fairy godfather's wand (or pen) of Mr. Andrew Lang. He, too, I think perhaps, cares more for the " epic " than the " ornamental " side of illustration ; he generally shows a pretty poetical fancy.

At the head, perhaps, of the newer school of decorative illustrators ought to be named Mr. Robert Anning Bell, whose taste and feeling for style alone gives him a distinctive place. He has evidently studied the early printers and book-decorators in outline of Venice and Florence to some purpose; by no means merely imitatively, but with his own type of figure and face, and fresh natural impressions, observes with much taste

CHARLES RICKETTS.

FROM "DAPHNIS AND CHLOE." (THE VALE PRESS.)

and feeling for beauty the limitations and decorative suggestions in the relations of line-drawing and typography. Many of his designs to "The Midsummer Night's Dream" are delightful both as drawings and as decorative illustrations.

The newest book illustrator is perhaps Mr.

CONTEMPORARY ILLUSTRATORS.

Charles Robinson, whose work appears to be full of invention, though I have not yet had sufficient opportunities of doing it justice. He shows quaint and sometimes weird fancy, a love of fantastic

C. H. SHANNON.

FROM "DAPHNIS AND CHLOE." (THE VALE PRESS.)

architecture, and is not afraid of outline and large white spaces.

Mr. R. Spence shows considerable vigour and originality. He distinguished himself first by some pen drawings which won the gold medal at

the National Competitions at South Kensington, in which a romantic feeling and dramatic force was shown in designs of mediæval battles, expressed in forcible way, consistent with good line and effect in black and white. His design of the Legend of St. Cuthbert in "The Quarto" is perhaps the most striking thing he has done. I am enabled to print one of his characteristic designs of battles.

AUBREY BEARDSLEY.

FROM THE "MORTE D'ARTHUR." (DENT.)

Mr. A. Jones also distinguished himself about the same time as Mr. Spence in the National Competition, and showed some dramatic and romantic feeling. The design given shows a more ornamental side.

Mr. William Strang, who has made his mark in etching as a medium for designs full of strong character and weird imagination, also shows in his processed pen drawings vigorous line and perception of decorative value, as in the designs to "Munchausen," two of which are here reproduced.

The publication of "The Evergreen" by Patrick Geddes and his colleagues at Edinburgh has introduced several black and white designers of force and character—Mr. Robert Burns and Mr. John Duncan, for instance, more particularly distinguishing themselves for decorative treatment in which one may see the influences of much fresh inspiration from Nature.

Miss Mary Sargant Florence shows power and decorative feel-ing in her out-line designs to "The Crystal Ball." Mr. Granville Fell must be named among the new-er school of de-corative illus-trators; and Mr. Paul Wood-roffe, who also shows much facility of de-sign and feeling for old English life in his books of Nursery Rhymes; his re-cent work shows much refine-ment of drawing and feeling.

AUBREY BEARDSLEY.

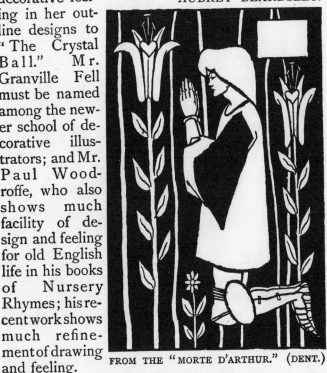

FROM THE "MORTE D'ARTHUR." (DENT.)

Miss Alice B. Woodward ought also to be named for her clever treatment of mediæval life in black and white.

More recently, perhaps the most remarkable work in book illustration has been that of Mr. E. J. Sullivan, whose powerful designs to

Carlyle's "Sartor Resartus" are full of vigour and character.

Force and character, again, seem the leading qualities in the striking work of another of our recent designers in black and white, Mr. Nicholson, who also engraves his own work.

EDMUND J. SULLIVAN.

FROM "SARTOR RESARTUS."　　　　　　(BELL.)

Mr. Gordon Craig adds printing to the crafts of black and white design and engraving, and has a distinctive feeling of his own.

The revival in England of decorative art of all kinds during the last five and twenty years, culminating as it appears to be doing in book-design, has not escaped the eyes of observant and

FROM THE PEN DRAWING.

THE HOUSE
OF JOY

By LAURENCE
HOUSMAN
London: KEGAN PAUL
TRENCH TRUBNER & Co

1895

TITLE-PAGE OF "THE HOUSE OF JOY." (KEGAN PAUL, 1895.)

FROM "FRANGILLA." (ELKIN MATHEWS.)

The·moon·
has·a·
face·like·
the·
clock·in
the·hall;

FROM "A CHILD'S GARDEN OF VERSE."   (LANE, 1895.)

CHARLES ROBINSON.

THE
CHILD
ALONE.

FROM "A CHILD'S GARDEN OF VERSE."   (LANE, 1895.)

237

THE ·COW·

FROM A "CHILD'S GARDEN OF VERSE." (LANE, 1895.)

sympathetic artists and writers upon the Continent. The work of English artists of this kind has been exhibited in Germany, in Holland, in Belgium and France, and has met with remarkable appreciation and sympathy.

In Belgium, particularly, where there appears to be a somewhat similar movement in art, the work

J. D. BATTEN.

FROM "THE ARABIAN NIGHTS."   (J. M. DENT AND CO.)

of the newer school of English designers has awakened the greatest interest. The fact that M. Oliver Georges Destrée has made sympathetic literary studies of the English pre-Raphaelites and their successors, is an indication of this. The exhibitions of the "XXᵉ Siècle," "La libre Æsthetique," at Brussels and Liège, are also evidence of the repute in which English designers are held.

THE CONTINENT.

In Holland, too, a special collection of the designs of English book illustrators has been exhibited at the Hague and other towns under the auspices of M. Loffelt.

At Paris, also, the critics and writers on art have

J. D. BATTEN.

FROM "THE ARABIAN NIGHTS."   (J. M. DENT AND CO.)

been busy in the various journals giving an account of the Arts and Crafts movement, the Kelmscott Press, and the school of English book-decorators in black and white, and the recent exhibitions of "L'Art Nouveau" and "Le Livre

242

FROM "A MIDSUMMER NIGHT'S DREAM."
(J. M. DENT AND CO., 1895.)

FROM "BEAUTY AND THE BEAST."
(J. M. DENT AND CO., 1894.)

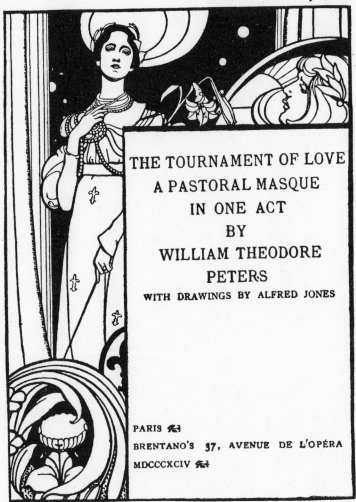

THE TOURNAMENT OF LOVE
A PASTORAL MASQUE
IN ONE ACT
BY
WILLIAM THEODORE
PETERS
WITH DRAWINGS BY ALFRED JONES

PARIS
BRENTANO'S 37, AVENUE DE L'OPÉRA
MDCCCXCIV

A TITLE-PAGE.

FROM "BARON MUNCHAUSEN."   (LAWRENCE AND BULLEN.)

Moderne" at Paris are further evidence of the interest taken there in English art.

Without any vain boasting, it is interesting to note that whereas most artistic movements affect-

WILLIAM STRANG.

FROM " MUNCHAUSEN " (LAWRENCE AND BULLEN).

ing England are commonly supposed to have been imported from the Continent, we are credited at last with a genuine home growth in artistic development. Although, regarded in the large sense, country or nationality is nothing to art (being at its best always cosmopolitan and international)

BELGIUM.
yet in the history of design, national and local
varieties, racial characteristics and local develop-

H. GRANVILLE FELL.

ments must
always have
their value
and historic
interest.

We may,
perhaps, take
it as a sympa-
thetic response
to English
feeling, the
appearance of
such books as
M. Rijsselber-
ghe's Alma-
nack, with its
charming de-
signs in line,
from the house
of Dietrich
at Brussels.
M. Fernand
Knopff's work,
original as it
is, shows sym-
pathy with the
later English
school of poetic
and decorative
design of which D. G. Rossetti may be said to
have been the father, though in book-illustration
proper I am not aware that he has done much.

254

FROM "THE EVERGREEN." (GEDDES AND CO., 1895.)

FROM "THE EVERGREEN."   (GEDDES AND CO., 1895.)

FROM "THE CRYSTAL BALL."   (BELL, 1894.)

FROM "SECOND BOOK OF NURSERY RHYMES." (GEORGE ALLEN, 1896.)

In Holland in black and white design there is
M. G. W. Dijsselhof and M. R. N. Roland Holst.

In Germany, such original and powerful artists
as Josef Sattler and Franz Stück; the former
seemingly inheriting much of the grim and stern
humour of the old German masters, as well as
their feeling for character and treatment of line,
while his own personality is quite distinct. While

PAUL WOODROFFE.

FROM "NURSERY RHYMES."   (BELL, 1895.)

Sattler is distinctly Gothic in sympathy, Stück
seems more to lean to the pagan or classical side,
and his centaurs and graces are drawn with much
feeling and character. We have already mentioned
the "Munich Calendar," designed by Otto Hupp,
which is well known for the vigour and spirit with
which the artist has worked after the old German manner, with bold treatment of heraldic devices, and has
effectively used colour with line work. The name
of Seitz appears upon some effectively designed
allegorical figures, one of Gutenberg at his press.

265

"JUGEND."

"Jugend," a copiously illustrated journal published at Munich by Dr. Hirth, shows that there are many clever artists with a more or less decorative aim in illustration, which in others seems rather overgrown with grotesque feeling and morbid extravagance, but there is an abundance of exuberant life, humour, whimsical fancy and spirit characteristic of South Germany.

M. RIJSSELBERGHE.

"Ver Sacrum," the journal of the group of the "Secession" artists of Vienna, gives evidence of considerable daring and resource in black and white drawing, though mainly of an impressionistic or pictorial aim.

M. Larisch, of Vienna, has distinguished himself by his works upon the artistic treatment and spacing of letters which contain examples of the work of different artists both continental and English.

French artists in decoration of all kinds have been so largely influenced or affected by the Japanese, and have so generally approached design from the impressionistic, dramatic, or accidental-individualist point of view, that the somewhat severe limits imposed by a careful taste in all art with an ornamental purpose, does not appear to have greatly attracted them. At all times it would seem that the dramatic element is the dominant one in French art, and this, though of course quite reconcilable with the ornament instinct, is seldom found perfectly united with it, and, where present, generally gets the upper hand. The older classical or Renaissance ornamental feeling of designers like Galland and Puvis de Chavannes seems to be dying out, and the modern *chic* and daring of a Cheret seems to be more characteristic of the moment.

Yet, on the other hand, among the newer French School, we find an artist of such careful methods and of such strong decorative instinct as Grasset, on what I should call the architectural side in contradistinction to the impressionistic. His work, though quite characteristically French in spirit and sentiment, is much more akin in method to our English decorative school. In fact, many of Grasset's designs suggest that he has done what our men have done, studied the art of the middle ages from the remains in his own country, and grafted upon this stock the equipment and sentiment of a modern.

In his book illustrations he seems, however, so far as I know, to lean rather towards illustrations pure and simple, rather than decoration, and exhibits great archæological resource as well as romantic feeling in such designs as those to " Les Cinq Fils d'Aymon." The absence of book decoration in the English sense, in France, however, may be due to the want of beauty or artistic feeling in the typographer's part of the work. Modern French type has generally assumed elongated and meagre forms which are not suggestive of rich decorative effect, and do not combine with design : nor, so far as I have been able to observe, does there seem to be any feeling amongst the designers for the artistic value of lettering, or any serious attempt to cultivate better forms. The poster-artist, to whom one would think, being essential to his work, the value of lettering in good forms would appeal, generally tears the roman alphabet to tatters, or uses extremely debased and ugly varieties.

More recently, however, French designers and printers appear to be giving attention to the subject, and newly designed types are appearing ; one firm at Paris having issued a fount designed by Eugene Grasset.

The charming designs of Boutet de Monvel should be named as among the most distinctive of modern French book illustrations, for their careful drawing and decorative effect, although, being in colours, they hardly belong to the same category as the works we have been considering, and the relation of type to pictures leaves something to be desired.

A respect for form and style in lettering, is, I take it, one of the most unmistakable indications of a good decorative sense. A true ornamental

instinct can produce a fine ornamental effect by
means of a mass of good type or MS. lettering
WALTER CRANE.

FROM SPENSER'S "FAERIE QUEENE."
(GEORGE ALLEN, 1896.)

alone: and considered as accompaniments
or accessories to design they are invalu-
able, as presenting opportunites of contrast or recurrence in mass or line to other
elements in the composition. To the
decorative illustrator of books they are
the unit or primal element from which
he starts.

The publication at Venice of " L'Arte
della stampa nel Renascimento Italiano
Venezia," by Ferd. Ongania—a series of
reproductions of woodcuts, ornaments, initials,
title-pages, etc., from some of the choicest of the
books of the early Venetian and Florentine

printers, may perhaps be taken as a sign of the growth of a similar interest in book decoration in that country, unless, like other works, it is intended chiefly for the foreign visitor.

A sumptuously printed quarterly on Art, which has of late made its appearance at Rome, " Il Convito," seems to show an interest in the decorative side, and does not confine its note on illustrations to Italian work, but gives reproductions from the works of D. G. Rossetti, and from Elihu Vedder's designs to " The Rubaiyat of Omar Khayyam."

Certainly if the possession of untold treasures of endlessly beautiful invention in decorative art, and the tradition of ancient schools tend to foster and to stimulate original effort, one would think that it should be easier for Italian artists than those of other countries to revive something of the former decorative beauty of the work of her printers and designers in the days of Aldus and Ratdolt, of the Bellini and Botticelli.

It does not appear to be enough, however, to possess the seed merely ; or else one might say that where a museum is, there will the creative art spring also ; it is necessary to have the soil also ; to plough and sow, and then to possess our souls in patience a long while ere the new crop appears, and ere it ripens and falls to our sickle. It is only another way of saying, that art is the outcome of life, not of death.

Artists may take motives or inspiration from the past, or from the present, it matters not, so long as their work has life and beauty—so long as it is organic, in short.

FROM "OTTO OF THE SILVER HAND."   (SCRIBNER.)

I have already alluded to the movement in Boston among a group of cultured young men— Mr. Lee the printer and his colleagues—more or less inspired by " The Hobby Horse" and the Kelmscott Press, which resulted in the printing of " The Knight Errant."

Some years before, however, Mr. Howard Pyle distinguished himself as a decorative artist in book designs, which showed, among other more modern

FROM " OTTO OF THE SILVER HAND." (SCRIBNER.)

influences, a considerable study of the method of Albert Dürer. I give a reproduction which suggests somewhat the effect of the famous copperplate of Erasmus. He sometimes uses a lighter method, such as is shown in the drawings to " The One Horse Shay."

Of late in his drawings in the magazines, Mr. Pyle has adopted the modern wash method, or painting in black and white, in which, however able in its own way, it is distinctly at a considerable loss of individuality and decorative interest.[1]

Another artist of considerable invention and

WILL. H. BRADLEY.

A COVER DESIGN. (CHICAGO, 1894.)

decorative ability has recently appeared in

[1] I am informed that the adoption of the wash method is not recent with Mr. Pyle, but that he adapts his method to his matter. This does not, however, affect the opinion expressed as to the relative artistic value of wash and line work.

WILL. H. BRADLEY.

PROSPECTUS OF "BRADLEY HIS BOOK."
(SPRINGFIELD, MASS., 1896.)

DESIGN FOR "THE CHAP-BOOK."   (CHICAGO, 1895.)

AMERICAN ARTISTS.

America, Mr. Will. H. Bradley, whose designs for
" The Inland Printer" of Chicago are remarkable
for careful and delicate line-work, and effective
treatment of black and white, and showing the
influence of the newer English school with a
Japanese blend

CHAPTER V. OF GENERAL PRINCIPLES IN DESIGNING BOOK ORNAMENTS AND ILLUSTRATIONS: CONSIDERATIONS OF ARRANGEMENT, SPACING, AND TREATMENT.

IT may not be amiss to add a few words as a kind of summary of general principles to which we seem to be naturally led by the line of thought I have been pursuing on this subject of book decoration.

As I have said, there is nothing final or absolute in Design. It is a matter of continual re-arrangement, re-adjustment, and modification or even transformation of certain elements. A kind of imaginative chemistry of forms, masses, lines, and quantities, continually evolving new combinations. But each artistic problem must be solved on its merits, and as each one varies and presents fresh questions, it follows that no absolute rules or principles can be laid down to fit particular cases, although as the result of, and evolved out of, practice, certain general guiding principles are valuable, as charts and compasses by which the designer can to a certain extent direct his course.

To begin with, the enormous variety in style, aim, and size of books, makes the application of definite principles difficult. One must narrow the problem down to a particular book, of a given character and size.

Apart from the necessarily entirely personal and individual questions of selection of subject, motive, feeling or sentiment, consider the conditions

279

of the book-page. Take an octavo page—such as one of those of this volume.

Although we may take the open book with the double-columns as the page proper, in treating a book for illustration, we shall be called upon sometimes to treat them as single pages. But whether single or double, each has its limits in the mass of type forming the full page or column which gives the dimensions of the designer's panel. The whole or any part of this panel may be occupied by design, and one principle of procedure in the ornamental treatment of a book is to consider any of the territory not occupied by the type as a fair field for accompanying or terminating design—as, for instance, at the ends of chapters, where more or less of the type page is left blank.

Unless we are designing our own type, or drawing our lettering as a part of the design, the character and form of the type will give us a sort of gauge of degree, or key, to start with, as to the force of the black and white effect of our accompanying designs and ornaments. For instance, one would generally avoid using heavy blacks and thick lines with a light open kind of type, or light open work with very heavy type. (Even here one must qualify, however, since light open penwork has a fine and rich effect with black letters sometimes.)

My own feeling—and designing must always finally be a question of individual feeling—is rather to acknowledge the rectangular character of the type page in the shape of the design ; even in a vignette, by making certain lines extend to the limits, so as to convey a feeling of rectangular

SACRED hunger of ambitious mindes,
And impotent desire of men to raine !
Whom neither dread of God, that devils bindes,
Nor lawes of men, that common-weales containe,
Nor bands of nature, that wilde beastes restraine,
Can keepe from outrage and from doing wrong,
Where they may hope a kingdome to obtaine :
No faith so firme, no trust can be so strong,
No love so lasting then, that may enduren long.

Witnesse may Burbon be ; whom all the bands
Which may a Knight assure had surely bound,
Untill the love of Lordship and of lands
Made him become most faithless and unsound :
And witnesse be Gerioneo found,
Who for like cause faire Belgè did oppresse,
And right and wrong most cruelly confound :
And so be now Grantorto, who no lesse
Then all the rest burst out to all outragiousnesse.

FROM SPENSER'S "FAERIE QUEENE."   (GEORGE ALLEN, 1896.)

WALTER CRANE.

FROM SPENSER'S "FAERIE QUEENE."   (GEORGE ALLEN, 1896.)

283

Britomart chaceth Ollyphant;
Findes Scudamour distrest:
Assayes the house of Busyrane,
Where Loues spoyles are represt.

ROM SPENSER'S "FAERIE QUEENE."   (GEORGE ALLEN, 1896.)

control and compactness, as in the tail-piece given here from " The Faerie Queene."

But first, if one may, paradoxically, begin with " end paper" as it is curiously called, there is the lining of the book. Here the problem is to cover two leaves entirely in a suggestive and agreeable, but not obtrusive way. One way is to design a repeating pattern much on the principle of a small printed textile, or miniature wall-paper, in one or more colours. Something delicately suggestive of the character and contents of the book is in place here, but nothing that competes with the illustrations proper. It may be considered as a kind of quadrangle, forecourt, or even a garden or grass plot before the door.

We are not intended to linger long here, but ought to get some hint or encouragement to go on into the book. The arms of the owner (if he is fond of heraldry, and wants to remind the potential book borrower to piously return) may appear hereon—the book-plate.

If we are to be playful and lavish, if the book is for Christmastide or for children, we may catch a sort of fleeting butterfly idea on the fly-leaves before we are brought with becoming, though dignified curiosity, to a short pause at the half-title. Having read this, we are supposed to pass on with somewhat bated breath until we come to the double doors, and the front and full title are disclosed in all their splendour.

Even here, though, the whole secret of the book should not be let out, but rather played with or suggested in a symbolic way, especially in any ornament on the title-page, in which the lettering should be the chief ornamental feature. A frontispiece may be more pictorial in treatment if desired, and it is reasonable to occupy the whole of the type page both for the lettering of title and the picture in the front; then, if richness of effect is desired, the margin may be covered also almost to the edge of the paper by inclosing borders, the width of these borders varying according to the varying width of the paper margin, and in the same proportions, *recto* and *verso* as the case may be, the broad side turning outwards to the edge of the book each way.

This is a plan adopted in the opening of the Kelmscott books, of which that of " The Glittering Plain," given here, may be taken as a type. Though Mr. Morris places his title page on the left to face the opening of first chapter, and does not use a frontispiece, he obtains a remarkably rich and varied effect of black and white in his larger title pages by placing in his centre panel strong black Gothic letters; or, as in the case of the Kelmscott Chaucer, letters in white relief upon a floral arabesque adapted to the space, and filling the field with a lighter floral network in open line, and enclosing this again with the rich black and white marginal border.

If I may refer again to my own work, in the designs to "The Faerie Queene" the full-page designs are all treated as panels of figure design, or pictures, and are enclosed in fanciful borders, in which subsidiary incidents of characters of the poem are introduced or suggested, somewhat on the plan of mediæval tapestries. A reduction of one of these is given above.

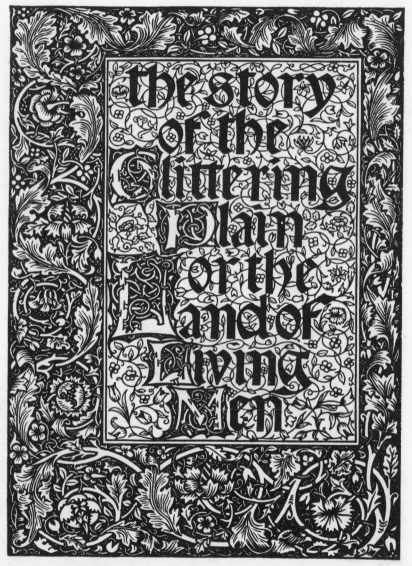

The Story of the Glittering Plain or the Land of Living Men

FROM "THE STORY OF THE GLITTERING PLAIN."

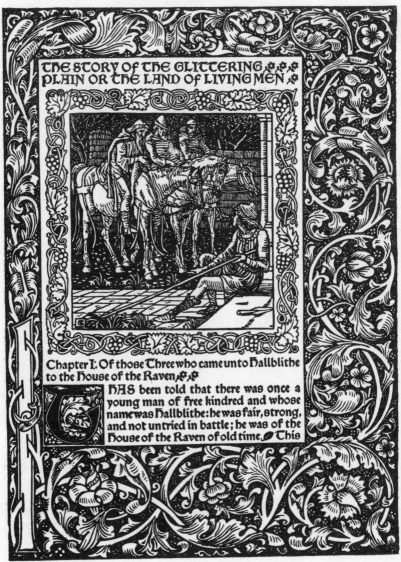

THE STORY OF THE GLITTERING PLAIN OR THE LAND OF LIVING MEN

Chapter I. Of those Three who came unto Hallblithe to the House of the Raven.

HAS been told that there was once a young man of free kindred and whose name was Hallblithe: he was fair, strong, and not untried in battle; he was of the House of the Raven of old time. This

A full-page design may, thus inclosed and separated from the type pages, bear carrying considerably further, and be more realized and stronger in effect than the ornaments of the type page, just as in the illuminated MSS. highly wrought miniatures were worked into inclosing borders on the centres of large initial letters, which formed a broad framework, branching into light floral scroll or leaves upon the margin and uniting with the lettering.

Much depends upon the decorative scheme. With appropriate type, a charming, simple, and broad effect can be obtained by using outline alone, both for the figure designs or pictures, and the ornament proper.

The famous designs of the "Hypnerotomachia Poliphili," 1499, may be taken as an instance of this treatment; also the "Fasciculus Medicinæ," 1495, "Æsop's Fables," 1493, and other books of the Venetian printers of about this date or earlier, which are generally remarkable for fine quality of their outline and the refinement and grace of their ornaments.

One of the most effective black and white page borders of a purely ornamental kind is one dated 1478, inclosing a page of Roman type, (see illustration, Venice, 1478, Pomponius Mela). A meandering arabesque of a rose-stem leaf and flower, white on a black ground, springing from a circle in the broad margin at the bottom, in which are two shields of arms. A tolerably well known but most valuable example.

The opening chapter of a book affords an opportunity to the designer of producing a decorative effect by uniting ornament with type. He can place figure design in a frieze-shaped panel (say of about a fourth of the page) for the heading, and weight it by a bold initial letter designed in a square, from which may spring the stem and leaves of an arabesque throwing the letter into relief, and perhaps climbing up and down the margin, and connecting the heading with the initial. The initialed page from "The Faerie Queene" is given as an example of such treatment. The title, or any chapter inscription, if embodied in the design of the heading, has a good effect.

Harmony between type and illustration and ornament can never, of course, be quite so complete as when the lettering is designed and drawn as a part of the whole, unless the type is designed by the artist. It entails an amount of careful and patient labour (unless the inscriptions are very brief) few would be prepared to face, and would mean, practically, a return to the principle of the block book.

Even in these days, however, books have been entirely produced by hand, and, for that matter, if beauty were the sole object, we could not do better than follow the methods of the scribe, illuminator, and miniaturist of the Middle Ages. But the world clamours for many copies (at least in some cases), and the artist must make terms with the printing press if he desires to live. It would be a delightful thing if every book were different—a millennium for collectors! Perhaps, too, it might be a wholesome regulation at this stage if authors were to qualify as scribes (in the old sense) and

KETHAM'S "FASCICULUS MEDICINÆ." (VENICE, DE GREGORIIS, 1493.)

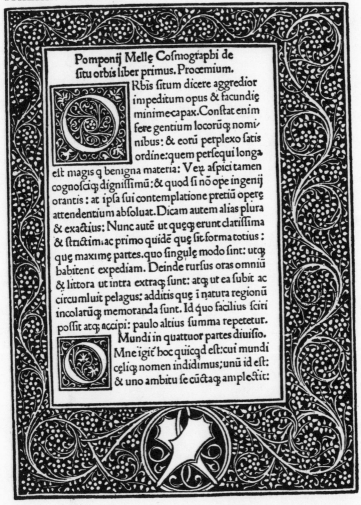

POMPONIUS MELA. (VENICE, RATDOLT, 1478.)

write out their own works in beautiful letters! How it would purify literary style!

There is no doubt that great attention has been given to the formation of letters by designers in the past.

Albrecht Dürer, in his "Geometrica," for instance, gives an elaborate system for drawing the Roman capitals, and certainly produces by its means a fine alphabet in that type of letter, apparently copied from ancient Roman inscriptions. He does the same for the black letters also.[1]

For the Roman capitals he takes a square, and divides it into four equal parts for the A. The horizontal line across the centre gives the crossbar. The sides of the square are divided into eighths, and one eighth is measured at the top of vertical dividing line, one eighth again from each bottom corner of the square to these points, the limbs of the A, are drawn; the up stroke and cross-bar being one-sixteenth, the down stroke being one-eighth of the square in thickness. Circles of one-fourth of the square in diameter are struck at the top of the A where the limbs meet, and at lower corners, to form the outside serifs of the feet, the inside serifs being formed by circles of one-sixteenth diameter; and so the A is complete. Various sub-divisions of the square are given as guides in the formation of the other letters less symmetrical, and two or three forms are given of some, such as the O, and the R, Q, and S; but the same proportions of thick and thin strokes are adhered to, and the same method of forming the serifs.

[1] Reproduced in "Alphabets," by E. F. Strange (pp. 244-250), Ex-Libris Series. Bell.

THE DÜRER ALPHABETS.

For the black letter (lower case German) text the proportions are five squares for the short letters i, n, m, u, the space between the strokes of a letter like u being one-third the thickness of the stroke, the top and bottom one being covered with one square, set diamond-wise. Eight squares for the long letters l, h, b ; the tops cut off diagonally, the feet turned diamond-wise.

This is interesting as showing the care and sense of proportion which may be expended upon the formation of lettering. It also gives a definite standard. The division of eighths and fourths in the Roman capital is noteworthy, too, in connection with the eight-heads standard of proportion for the human body ; and the square basis reminds one of Vitruvius, and demonstration of the inclosure of the human figure with limbs in extension by the square and the circle.

Those interested in the history of the form of lettering cannot do better than consult Mr. Strange's book on "Alphabets" in this series.

It might be possible to construct an actual theory of the geometric relation of figure design, ornamental forms, and the forms of lettering, text, or type upon them, but we are more concerned with the free artistic invention for the absence of which no geometric rules can compensate. The invention, the design, comes first in order, the rules and principles are discovered afterwards, to confirm and establish their truth—would that they did not also sometimes crystallize their vitality !

I have spoken of the treatment of headings and initials at the opening of a chapter. In deciding upon such an arrangement the designer is more or less committed to carrying it out throughout the book, and would do well to make his ornamental spaces, and the character, treatment, and size of his initials agree in the corresponding places. This would still leave plenty of room for variety of invention in the details.

The next variety of shape in which he might indulge would be the half-page, generally an attractive proportion for a figure design, and if repeated on the opposite page or column, the effect of a continuous frieze can be given, which is very useful where a procession of figures is concerned, and the slight break made by the centre margin is not objectionable.

The same plan may be adopted when it is desired to carry a full-page design across, or meet it by a corresponding design opposite.

Then we come to the space at the end of the chapter. For my part, I can never resist the opportunity for a tailpiece if it is to be a fully illustrated work, though some would let it severely alone, or be glad of the blank space to rest a bit. I think this lets one down at the end of the chapter too suddenly. The blank, the silence, seems too dead ; one would be glad of some lingering echo, some recurring thought suggested by the text ; and here is the designer's opportunity. It is a tight place, like the person who is expected to say the exactly fit thing at the right moment. Neither too much, or too little. A quick wit and a light hand will serve the artist in good stead here.

Page-terminations or tailpieces may of course be very various in plan, and their style correspond with or be a variant of the style of the rest of the decorations of the book. Certain types are apt to recur, but while the bases may be similar, the superstructure of fancy may vary as much as we like. There is what I should call the mouse-tail termination, formed on a gradually diminishing line, starting the width of the type, and ending in a point. Printers have done it with dwindling lines of type, finishing with a single word or an aldine leaf.

Then there is the plan of boldly shutting the gate, so to speak, by carrying a panel of design right across, or filling the whole of the remaining page. This is more in the nature of additional illustration to carry on the story, and might either be a narrow frieze-like strip, or a half, or three-quarter page design as the space would suggest.

There is the inverted triangular plan, and the shield or hatchment form. The garland or the spray, sprig, leaf, or spot, or the pen flourish glorified into an arabesque.

The medallion form, or seal shape, too, often lends itself appropriately to end a chapter with, where an inclosed figure or symbol is wanted. One principle in designing isolated ornaments is useful : to arrange the subject so that its edges shall touch a graceful boundary, or inclosing shape, whether the boundary is actually defined by inclosing lines or frame-work or not. Floral, leaf, and escutcheon shapes are generally the best, but free, not rigidly geometrical. The value of a certain economy of line can hardly be too much appreciated, and the perception of the necessity of recurrence of line, and a re-echoing in the details of leading motives in line and mass. It is largely upon such small threads that decorative success and harmonious effect depend, and they are particularly closely connected with the harmonious disposition of type and ornamental illustration which we have been considering.

It would be easy to fill volumes with elaborate analysis of existing designs from this point of view, but designs, to those who feel them, ought to speak in their own tongue for themselves more forcibly than any written explanation or commentary; and, though of making of many books there is no end, every book must have its end, even though that end to the writer, at least, may seem to leave one but at the beginning.

FROM "GOOD WORDS FOR THE YOUNG."   (STRAHAN, 1871.)

Chap. IV. Of the Recent Development, etc., p. 189. In addition to the names of the modern printers and presses mentioned in this chapter must now be added those of several workers in the field of artistic printing who have distinguished themselves since the Kelmscott Press.

Mr. Cobden Sanderson has turned from the outside adornment of the book to the inside, and, in association with Mr. Emery Walker, whose technical knowledge and taste was so valuable on the Kelmscott Press, has founded " The Doves Press " at Hammersmith, and has issued books remarkable for the pure severity of their typography, founded mainly upon Jenson.

Mr. St. John Hornby also must be named, more particularly for his revival of a very beautiful Italian type founded upon the type of Sweynheim and Pannartz, the first printers in Italy. The Greek type designed by the late Robert Proctor, based on the Alcala fount used in the New Testament of the Complutensian Polyglot Bible of 1514, should be mentioned as the only modern attempt to improve the printing of Greek, with the exception of Mr. Selwyn Image's, which perhaps suffered by being cut very small to suit commercial exigences.

Mr. C. R. Ashbee, too, has established a very extensive printery, " The Essex House Press," which he has since transplanted to Chipping Camden. He had the assistance of several of the workers from the Kelmscott Press, and has produced many excellently printed books of late years, such as the Benvenuto Cellini, and including such elaborate productions as Edward VI.'s Prayer Book, with wood-engravings and initials and ornaments as well as the type of his own design.

An interesting series of the English poets, also, with frontispieces by various artists, has been issued from this press.

P. 218.   The death of Aubrey Beardsley since the notice of his work was written must be recorded, and it would seem as if the loss of this extraordinary artist marked the decadence of our modern decadents.

A perhaps equally remarkable designer, however, whose work has a certain kinship in some features with Beardsley's, is Mr. James Syme, whose work has not before been noticed in this book. He has a powerful and weird imagination associated with grotesque and satirical design, and considerable skill in the use of line and black and white effect.

P. 267. In writing of book illustrators in France, a leading place should be given to M. Boutet de Monvel, whose delicate drawing, tasteful colouring, and sense of decorative effect, combined with abundant resource in variety of costume, and skilful treatment of crowds, mediaeval battle scenes, and ceremonial groups are seen to full advantage in his recent "Ste. Jean d'Arc," although no particular relationship between illustration and type is attempted.

P. 268.   A recent proof of the revival of taste in book-decoration and artistic printing in Italy may be referred to here as showing the influence of the English movement. I mean the edition of Gabriele d'Annunzio's "Francesca da Rimini" with illustrations or rather decorations by Adolphus de Karolis, printed by the Fratelli Treves in 1902.

This book shows unmistakable signs of study of recent English work, as well as of the early printers of Venice, and it is strange to think how sometimes artists of one country may come back to an appreciation of a particular period of their own historic art by the aid of foreign spectacles. Among the original designers of modern Italy may be mentioned G. M. Mataloni, who shows remarkable powers of draughtsmanship and invention, largely spent upon posters and ex-libris.

Italy, too, has an able critic and chronicler of the work of book-designers of all countries in Sig. Vittorio Pica of Naples, whose "Attraverso gli Albi e le Cartelle" (Istituto Italiano d'arti grafiche editore Bergamo) is very comprehensive.

In Vienna Prof. Larisch recently published a book of Alphabets designed by various artists of Europe; Germany, France, Italy, and England being represented. The group of Viennese artists known as the "Secession" have issued "Ver Sacrum," a monthly journal, or magazine, giving original designs of various artists more or less in the direction of book-decoration. Latterly the designs offered seemed to lose themselves either in an affectation of primitiveness and almost infantine simplicity, or the wildest grotesqueness and eccentricity.

APPENDIX.

HEADPIECE BY ALAN WRIGHT.

BOOK OF KELLS.   [See page 13.

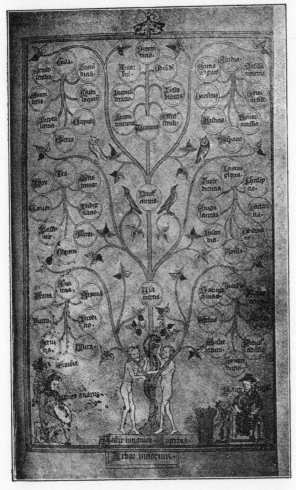

ARUNDEL PSALTER, 1339.

[See page 16.

ARUNDEL PSALTER, 1339. [See page 16.

ARUNDEL PSALTER, 1339.   [See page 16.

EPISTLE OF PHILIPPE DE COMINES TO RICHARD II.   [*See page* 23.

BEDFORD HOURS, PAGE OF CALENDAR, A.D. 1422.

[See page 23.

BEDFORD HOURS, A.D. 1422.   [See page 23.

ROMANCE OF THE ROSE.

[*See page* 29.

INITIAL LETTER, CHOIR BOOK, SIENA (1468—1472·3).   [*See page* 30.

HOKUSAI.   [*See page* 163.

HOKUSAI.   [*See page* 163.

INDEX.

ABBEY, Edwin, 166.
Æsop's Fables (Venice, 1493), 293.
—— (Ulm, 1498), 53.
—— (Naples, 1485), 55.
"Aglaia," cover for, 154, 157.
Alciati's Emblems, 109.
Aldus, 62, 63, 65, 108.
Alphabet (Dürer's), 299.
Alphabets (Bell, 1894), 299, 300.
Amman, Jost, 96.
American Wood-engraving, 148, 164.
Andersen's Fairy Tales (Allen, 1893), 199.
Anglo-Saxon MSS., 14, *et seq.*
Apocalypse, MS., 14th Cent., 19.
Arabian Nights (Dent, 1893), 241, 242.
Arndes, Steffen, 47.
Art in the House (Macmillan, 1876), 160, 162-165.
Arts and Crafts Exhibition Society, 207.
Arundel Psalter, MS., 16.
Aulus, Gellius (Venice, 1509), 73.

Bämler, 15.
Bateman, Robert, 160, 162-165.
Batten, J. D., 222, 241, 242.
Beardsley, Aubrey, 218, 221, 225, 226, 227.
Beauty and the Beast (Dent, 1894), 245.
Bedford Hours, MS., 23, 24, 38.

Beham, Hans Sebald, 96, 113.
Bell, R.A., 222, 243, 245.
Bellini, Giovanni, 62, 69.
Bernard, Solomon, 110.
Bewick, Thomas, 140, 145.
Bible (Cologne, 1480), 21.
—— (Lübeck, 1494), 47.
—— (Mainz, 1455), 49.
—— (Frankfort, 1563), 53, 131.
Bible Cuts (Holbein), 92, 95, 96.
Birmingham School, 203, 204, 207.
Blake, William, 136-139.
Block Books, 46.
Blomfield, Reginald, 207.
Boccaccio's *De Claris Mulieribus* (Ulm, 1473), 7, 11 ; (Ferrara, 1497), 54.
Bonhomme, 110.
Book of Carols (Allen, 1893), 209.
Books of Hours, 23, 24, 38, 54, 107.
Borders, 204, 293.
Bracebridge Hall (Macmillan, 1877), 158.
Bradley, Gertrude M., 207, 213.
—— Will. H., 274, 275, 277, 278.
Brown, Ford Madox, 154.
Buch von den Sieben Todsünden (Augsburg, 1474), 15.
Burgmair, Hans, 92, 95, 99, 101, 103, 105.
Burne-Jones, Sir Edward, 193.
Burns, Robert, 226, 259.

Caesenas, Stephanus, 59.
Caldecott, Randolph, 158.

INDEX.

Calepinus, Ambrosius, 121.

Calvert, Edward, 139-143.

"Card-Basket Style," The, 165.

Carroll, Lewis, 154.

Castle, Egerton, *English Book-plates*, 185.

Caxton, William, 49, 80.

Chaucer (Kelmscott Press, 1896), 193, 288.

Cheret, M., 267.

Child's Garden of Verse (Lane, 1895), 235, 237, 239.

Children's Books, 154, 156.

China, Early Printing in, 164.

Chiswick Press, The, 186.

Chodowiecki, D., 136.

Christ, Life of (Antwerp, 1487), 31.

Chroneken der Sassen (Mainz, 1492), 41.

Chronica Hungariæ (Augsburg, 1488), 35.

Cinderella (Dent, 1894), 254.

Cinq Fils d'Aymon, Les, 268.

Clark, R. and R., 186.

Columna, Francisco, 79.

Constable, T. and A., 186.

Contes Drolatiques, 150.

"Convito," Il, 270.

Copper-plate Engraving, 116, 129, 130.

"Cornhill," The, 172.

Cousin, Jean, 79.

Craig, Gordon, 228.

Cranach, Lucas, 95.

Crane, Walter, 174, 179, 181, 183, 191, 269, 281, 283, 285, 288, 290, 291.

Cremonese, P., 56.

Crystal Ball, The (Bell, 1894), 227, 261.

"Daily Chronicle," Illustrations in the, 165.

Dalziel Brothers, The, 150.

Dalziel's *Bible Gallery*, 152.

Dance of Death (Holbein's, 1538), 91, 92, 115.

Daniel, Rev. H., of Oxford, 189.

Dante, *Divina Commedia* MS., 10.

Dante (Venice, 1491), 56.

Daphnis and Chloe (Vale Press, 1893), 223, 224.

Davis, Louis, 170, 171.

Day, Lewis, 166.

De Claris Mulieribus (Ulm, 1473), 7, 11 ; (Ferrara, 1497), 54.

De Colines, Simon, 127.

De Gregoriis, 59, 295.

De Historia Stirpium (Basel, 1542), 119, 123.

Descent of Minerva, The (1508), 71.

Destrée, Oliver Georges, 241.

De Vinne Press, The, 189.

"Dial," The, 218.

Dictes and Sayings of the Philosophers (1477), 80.

Dijsselhof, G. W., 265.

Dinckmut, Conrad, 27.

Discovery of the Indies, The (Florence, 1493), 57.

Doré, Gustave, 149.

Duff, Gordon, *Early Printed Books*, 185.

Duncan, John, 226, 255, 257.

Du Pré, 54.

Dürer, Albrecht, 49, 80, 81, 83, 85, 87, 89, 95 ; his *Geometrica*, 294.

Early Italian Poets (Smith, Elder, 1861), 152.

Edgar, King, Newminster Charter, 14.

Emblem Books, 109, 110, 115, 116.

End-Papers, 285.

"English Illustrated Magazine," The, 170, 171, 173, 195.

Evans, Edmund, 156.

"Evergreen," The, 226, 255, 257, 259.

"Ex-Libris Series," The, 185.

Finé, Oronce, 91, 126, 127.

Fasciculus Medicinæ (Venice, 1495), 293.

Fell, H. Granville, 227, 254.

Feyrabend, Sigm., 131.

Fior di Virtù (Florence, 1493?), 58.

Flach, Martin, 108.

Flaxman, 136.

Flemish School, XVth Cent., 31.

Florence, Mary Sargant, 227, 261.

Ford, Henry, 222.

Formal Garden, The (Macmillan, 1892), 204, 205.

Foster, Birket, 150.

France, Modern Illustration in, 267.

Frangilla (Elkin Mathews, 1895), 233.

French MSS., 19, 37.

French School, XVth Cent., 37, 51, 126, 127.

Frontispieces, 286.

Froschover, 120.

Fuchsius, *De Historia Stirpium* (Basel, 1542), 119, 123.

Gaskin, Arthur, 199, 203.

—— Mrs., 203, 207.

Georgius de Rusconibus, 69, 75.

Gerard's Herbal, 120.

Gere, C. M., 195, 197, 203.

German School, XVth Cent., 3, 7, 11, 15, 17, 21, 25, 27, 35, 39, 41, 47, 53.

—— XVIth Cent., 81-117, 119, 131, 147.

Germany, Early Printing in, 46, 49.

—— Modern Illustration in, 172, 265.

Gesner, Conrad, 120.

Gilbert, John, 150.

Giolito, G., 133.

Giovio's Emblems, 116.

Girolamo da Cremona, 30.

Glittering Plain, The (Kelmscott Press, 1894), 191, 288, 289.

Goblin Market (Macmillan, 1862), 152.

"Good Words for the Young," 304.

Gospels, The, in Latin, MS., 14.

Grasset, M., 267, 268.

Greenaway, Kate, 158, 159.

Grimani Breviary, The, 29, 43, 45.

Grimm's Household Stories (Macmillan, 1882), 174, 179.

Grün, Hans Baldung, 96, 107, 108, 109, 110.

INDEX.

Halberstadt Bible, The, 49, 117.
Hardouyn, Gillet, 54, 107.
Harvey, William, 145.
Herbals, 16, 119, 120.
Hero and Leander (Vale Press, 1894), 219.
"Hobby Horse," The, 186, 270.
Hogarth, 135.
Hokusai, 163.
Holbein, Hans, 49, 80, 91, 92, 93, 95, 96, 115.
—— Ambrose, 92, 97.
Holiday, Henry, 154, 157.
Holland, Illustration in, 242, 265.
Holst, R. N. Roland, 265.
Horne, H. P., 186.
Hortulus Animæ (Strassburg, 1511), 107, 108, 109, 110.
Hortus Sanitatis (Mainz, 1491), 39.
House of Joy, The (Kegan Paul, 1895), 231.
Housman, Laurence, 222, 231.
Hughes, Arthur, 159-161, 304.
Hunt, Holman, 150.
Hunting of the Snark, The, (Macmillan, 1876), 154.
Huon of Bordeaux (Allen, 1895), 211.
Hupp, Otto, 174, 263.

Illuminated MSS., 5-10 *et seq.*
Image, Selwyn, 187, 189.
Indulgences (Mainz, 1454), 49.
"Inland Printer," The, 278.
Isingrin, Palma, 108, 119, 123.

Italian MSS., 10, 30.
Italian School, XVth Cent., 54-65.
—— —— XVIth Cent., 67-78, 121, 133.
Italy, Modern Illustration in, 268, 269.

Japan, Early Printing in, 163, 164.
Japanese Illustration, 156-164.
Jones, A. Garth, 226, 249.
"Jugend," 266.

Keene, Charles, 169, 172.
Kells, The Book of, 10, 13.
Kelmscott Press, The, 189, 190, 193, 194, 288, 290, 291.
Kerver, Thielman, 54, 79, 107.
King Wenceslas, 203.
Kleine Passion, Die (1512), 80, 81, 83, 85.
"Knight Errant," The (Boston), 189, 273.
Knopff, Fernand, 254.
Kreuterbuch (Strasburg, 1551), 120.

Larisch, M., 266.
Lawless, M. J., 172, 177.
Leeu, Gheraert, 31.
Leiden Christi (Bamberg, 1470), 3, 53.
Leighton, Sir Frederic, 152.
Lettering, 268.
Levetus, Celia, 207, 217.
Liberale da Verona, 30.
Linnell, John, 140.
Linton, W. J., 146-149, 151.
Lübeck Bible, The, 47.

338

Macdonald's *At the Back of the North Wind* (Strahan, 1871), 159-161.

Mainz, Early Printing at, 49.
—— Indulgences, The, 49.
—— Psalter, The, 50, 51.

Margins, 194.

Marks, H. S., 156.

Mason, F., 207, 211.

Matthiolus, 120.

Mazarine Bible, The, 49.

Meerfahrt zu Viln Onerkennten Inseln (Augsburg, 1509), 105.

Meidenbach, Jacob, 39.

Menzel, Adolf, 172.

Mer des Histoires, La, MS., 37.

Midsummer Night's Dream, A (Dent, 1895), 223, 243.

Millais, Sir J. E., 150.

Milton's Ode on Christ's Nativity (Nisbet, 1867), 155.

Minuziano, Alessandro, 67.

Missals, 29.

Monte Santo di Dio, El (Florence, 1477), 119.

Monvel, Boutet de, 268.

Moore, Albert, 154, 155.

Moore, Sturge, 218.

Morris, William, 189, 191, 193, 194, 288, 290, 291.

Morte D'Arthur (Dent, 1893), 221, 225, 227, 228.

Mother Goose (Routledge), 159.

Muckley, L. Fairfax, 222, 233.

Munchausen, Baron (Lawrence and Bullen, 1894), 226, 251, 253.

Neues Testament (Basel, 1523), 97.

New, Edmund H., 201, 203, 207.

Newill, Mary, 207, 215.

Newminster, Charter of Foundation of, MS. 14.

Niccolo di Lorenza, 119.

Nicholson, W., 228.

Northcote's *Fables,* 145.

Nursery Rhymes (Bell, 1894 : Allen, 1896), 227, 263, 265.

Omar Khayyam, 166.

"Once a Week," 169, 172, 175, 177.

Ongania, Ferd., 269.

Otmar, Johann, 145, 147.

Ottaviano dei Petrucci, 77.

Paganini, Alex., 121.

Palmer, Samuel, 140.

Papstthum mit sienen Gliedern (Nuremberg, 1526), 113.

Paris et Vienne, 1495, 51.

Parsons, Alfred, 166.

Payne, Henry, 207, 209.

Peard's *Stories for Children* (Allen, 1896), 167, 170.

Pennell, Joseph, 165, 185, 221.

Petri, Adam, 91, 107.

Pfister, Albrecht, 3, 53.

Philip le Noir, 108.

Philippe de Comines, Epistle of, MS., 23.

Photography, influence of, 174, 178.

Pierre le Rouge, 37.

Pigouchet, 54.

Pletsch, Oscar, 174.

Pliny's *Natural History* (Frankfort, 1582), 103.

INDEX.

Plutarchus Chæroneus (1513), 87 ; (1523), 89.
Poliphili Hypnerotomachia (1499), 62, 63, 65, 293.
——, French Edition, 79.
Pollard, A. W., *Early Illustrated Books*, 185.
Pomerium de Tempore (Augsburg, 1502), 147.
Pomponious Mela, 293, 297.
Poynter, E. J., 152.
Pre-Raphaelites, The, 150.
Princess Fiorimonde, Necklace of (Macmillan, 1880), 174, 181.
Printers' Marks, 96.
Psalters, MSS., 16, 20, 24.
Psalter (Mainz, 1457), 50, 51.
"Punch," 170, 172.
Pyle, Howard, 271, 273, 274.

Quadrupeds, History of (Zurich, 1554), 120.
Quarles' Emblems, 115, 116.
"Quarto," The, 226.
Quatriregio, 71.
Queen Mary's Psalter, MS., 20.
Quentel, Heinrich, 21.
"Quest," The, 203.
Quintilian (Venice, 1512), 75.

Ratdolt, Erhardt, 35, 297.
Reformation der bayrischen Landrecht (*Munich*, 1518), 116.
Renaissance, The, 61.
René of Anjou, Book of Hours of, 38.
Rethel, Alfred, 172.
Ricketts, C. S., 218, 219, 223.
Rijsselberghe, M., 254, 266.

Robinson, Charles, 222, 224, 235, 237, 239.
Rogers' *Poems*, 136, 146.
—— *Italy*, 136, 146.
Romance of the Rose, MS., 29, 43.
Rossetti, Christina, 152.
Rossetti, D. G., 150, 153.
Rylands, Henry, 173.

Sambourne, Linley, 170.
Sandys, Frederick, 172, 175.
Sartor Resartus (Bell, 1898), 228.
Sattler, Josef, 265.
Savage, Reginald, 218.
"Savoy," The, 221.
Schöffer, P., 41, 49, 50.
Schürer, Mathias, 111.
Schwind, M., 172.
"Scottish Art Review," The, 187.
Seitz, Professor A., 265.
Shannon, C. H., 218, 224.
Siena, Choir Books of, 30, 43, 45.
Sirens Three, The (Macmillan, 1886), 183.
Sleigh, Bernard, 207.
Smith, Winifred, 207.
Songs of Innocence (1789), 137.
Speculum Humanæ Vitæ (Augsburg, 1475), 17.
Spence, R., 224, 247.
Spenser's Faerie Queene (Allen, 1896), 269, 281, 283, 285, 288, 294.
Spiegel onser Behoudenisse (Kuilenburg, 1483), 25.
Steyner, Heinrich, 87.
Stothard, Thomas, 136, 146.
Strang, William, 226, 251, 253.

Strange, E. F., *Alphabets*, 185, 300.
Stück, Franz, 265.
"Studio," The, 221.
Sullivan, E. J., 227, 228.
Sumner, Heywood, 166, 167, 171.

Tacuino, Giov., 73.
Tail-pieces, 301.
Talbot Prayer-book, The, 26.
Tenison Psalter, The, MS., 16, 38.
Tenniel, Sir John, 150.
Tennyson's *Poems* (Moxon, 1857), 150, 151.
Terence, *Eunuchus*, German translation (Ulm, 1486), 27.
Thomas, F. Inigo, 204, 205, 207.
Title Page, development of the, 80.
Tory, Geoffroy, 126.
Tournament of Love, The (Paris, 1894), 249.
Treperel, Jehan, 51.
Triumphs of Maximilian, The, 95.
Tuppo's Æsop, 1485, 55.

Tuppo's Æsop, 1485, 55.
Turner, J. M. W., 146.
Type as affecting design, 267, 280, 294.

Vedder, Elihu, 166.
Veldener, Jan, 25.
Ver Sacrum, 266.
Vérard, 54.
Virgil Solis, 131.

Wächtlin, Hans, 96, 111.
Walton's "Angler" (Lane, 1896), 204.
Wandereisen, Hans, 113.
Weiss König, Der (1512-14), 95, 99.
White, Gleeson, 221.
Wilson, Patten, 221, 229.
Witney's Emblems, 116.
Wood-Engraving, Masters of (1889), 149.
Woodroffe, Paul, 227, 263, 265.
Woodward, Alice B., 227.

Zainer, Johann, 7, 11.
—— Günther, 17.

HEADPIECE BY ALAN WRIGHT.

341